Limping Through Forgiveness
A Journey Into Freedom

by Zdenka N. Slama

Forgiveness is the key to inner peace. Forgiving is only for the brave— for those willing to confront their pain and accept themselves as permanently changed.

Beverly Flanigan

Whether you turn to the right or to the left, your ears will hear a voice behind you, saying, "This is the way; walk in it." Isaiah 30:21.

LIMPING *through* FORGIVENESS

A JOURNEY INTO FREEDOM

Zdenka N. Slama

PUBLISHING

Belleville, Ontario, Canada

LIMPING THROUGH FORGIVENESS
Copyright © 2015, Zdenka N. Slama

All Rights Reserved. No part of this publication may be reproduced, stored in a retrieval system or transmitted in any form or by any means—electronic, mechanical, photocopy, recording or any other— except for brief quotations in printed reviews, without the prior permission of the author.

All Scripture quotations, unless otherwise specified, are from the HOLY BIBLE, NEW INTERNATIONAL VERSION ®. Copyright © 1973, 1978, 1984 by International Bible Society. Used by permission of Zondervan Publishing House. All rights reserved. Scripture quotations marked TLB are taken from *The Living Bible*. Copyright © 1971 by Tyndale House Publishers, Wheaton, Illinois 60187. All rights reserved. Scripture quotations marked NKJV are taken from the New King James Version. Copyright © 1979, 1980, 1982. Thomas Nelson Inc., Publishers. Scriptures marked NCV are taken from the New Century Version®. Copyright © 2005 by Thomas Nelson, Inc. Used by permission. All rights reserved.

Cataloguing data available from Library and Archives Canada

ISBN: 978-1-4600-0455-5
LSI Edition: 978-1-4600-0456-2
E-book ISBN: 978-1-4600-0457-9
(E-book available from the Kindle Store, KOBO and the iBooks Store)

Essence Publishing is a Christian Book Publisher dedicated to furthering the work of Christ through the written word. For more information, contact: 20 Hanna Court, Belleville, Ontario, Canada K8P 5J2
Phone: 1-800-238-6376. Fax: (613) 962-3055
Email: info@essence-publishing.com
Web site: www.essence-publishing.com

Dedication

I dedicate this book to my sister,
Anna,
As a small token of appreciation for the tender, unfailing
love and care she gave to our parents,
And as a legacy to our children,
Claudia and **Craig**,
And their families.

Table of Contents

Acknowledgements 9
"The Garden" by Suzanne Miller 11
Forewords 13
Preface 17

Section A: Admitting
 1   Bitter? Who, Me? 21
 2   The Fights 27
 3   The Effects of Violence and Abuse 31
 4   Navigating Life's Stormy Seas .35
 5   God Behind the Scenes 39
 6   The Escape 47
 7   Freedom 55
 8   A Separation 63

Section B: Becoming
 9   Learning to Forgive—Learning to Love 69

Section C: Constructing
 10 Forgetting What's Behind, Reaching for
     What's Ahead 81
 11 Packing My Suitcase Again 89
 12 Departure 93
 13 Tracking the Days 97
 14 Just As I Am 105
 15 Your Face I Seek 109
 16 A Night to Remember 113

Section D: Developing
   17 Mission Accomplished 121
   18 Love Overcomes 129
   19 Forgiveness for Me 135

Appendix: Stages of Forgiveness 147
   Stage A: Admitting 149
   Stage B: Becoming 151
   Stage C: Constructing 153
   Stage D: Developing 155

Acknowledgments

I owe the writing of this book to these women in my life: Claudia Scott, Michelle Delsaut, Ruth Willingham, Grace Adams and Ruth Muxworthy. My life wouldn't be what it is without them. I praise God for them.

My daughter, Claudia: Just because she was born! Later on she was there when my faith was drifting in a deep and stormy sea. She was there when I went back to school for my master's. She proofread my English papers and was always ready to discuss anything from theological issues to the history of Christianity and counselling strategies and theories. Claudia also did the last edit of this book before its submission to the publisher.

My oldest friend, Michelle: She was my first friend when I came to Canada. She was the first person to speak to me about God. Over the years she has proven to be a loyal friend. We have rejoiced and cried together over our children, supported one another in prayer and encouraged one another to keep on trusting even in the darkest night.

Our pastor Ted Willingham's wife, Ruth: Patiently, gently, she led me to Jesus Christ!

My friend Grace: I only met her once before approaching her with the belief that we should pray together for our families and our nation. Her name reminds me daily of God's grace to me. She was also the first one to do the rough edit of the whole book.

Lastly Ruth Muxworthy: She taught me to persist in prayer. After she learned about my parents, she continued to carry them on the wings of prayer long after I had given up on them.

Many thanks to our son, Craig Slama, and my friend Loreli Cockram for helping me with the book as much as time allowed them. And of course, where would I be without my husband, Peter, who always believes in me and who always sees me as better than I really am. Without his all-around support and love throughout the years this book could not have been written.

Thank you to Robert Bickle, Teresa Marchildon, Brian Cunnington, my beloved professor of counselling, and Brent Farquhar for their encouraging forewords. Thank you to Brenda Wood and Rose Harmer for their back cover contributions. Thank you to my friend Suzanne Miller for giving me permission to use her poem "The Garden."

Thank you to Glenis Mullings whose comment, "You sound bitter," started me on the road to self-discovery and completed forgiveness. This book would not have happened without him.

The Garden
by Suzanne Miller

Lord,
You speak—
and with Your Word breathe life
into Your amazing garden of humanity.
According to Your spoken design of us,
we flourish in different conditions of
shade and sunshine
coolness and heat—
with different measures of
water and pH balances needed for the soil of our souls.
Long and short seasons of life
You assign to us—
each one precious and purposeful to You.
Teach us to value
the intricate creation and the beauty of
each person,
encouraging each other to
discover and know the truth of
our own design—
that we may grow and blossom in the particular garden spot
You predestined for us.
As we daily surrender with
mind and heart
to the pruning and shaping of our will
to Yours—
we grow in understanding and knowledge of You
finding freedom and peace
glimpsing the eternal promise
of what it will be like living
with You
in
The Garden.

Forewords

In her autobiographical book of memoirs, Zdenka Slama chronicles her painful but at last liberating path to forgiveness. An arduous path fraught with pits and snares but assured nonetheless.

The idea of "limping through forgiveness" seems wrong, almost paradoxical. Aren't we to forgive and forget and to wipe the slate clean? In Christ, is not our yoke easy and our burden light? While this is true, notice that it is still is a yoke and a burden and there is still labour ahead. Jesus teaches that we must deny ourselves and take up our cross and follow Him. Indeed, the thought of Jesus stumbling up the road to Golgotha, carrying the cross of ultimate forgiveness, provides a vivid picture of how torturous the path to forgiveness can be. We are promised that we will not be given more than we can bear and that all things will work together for good, but we are not assured any easy road.

In Jeremiah 31:34 we read, "*For I will forgive their wickedness and will remember their sins no more*" (NIV). If this means our sins are literally forgotten and the slate wiped clean, why is the Bible not a clean slate? In fact, it reads like a journal of all the sordid details of God's chosen people, prophets and disciples. God's people, ultimately free and forgiven, but their transgressions not forgotten.

Is it even possible for an all-knowing God to have amnesia about anything, let alone our sins? No, it must be that we are acquitted and not condemned. In a legal sense, the record is clean. When we each day humbly seek His ways with a repentant heart, we are truly free and reckoned innocent. But still sometimes we limp home at day's end.

Throughout her staggering journey of forgiveness, Zdenka forgave, forgave again, and continues to forgive in a daily commitment to the road of redemption to redeem her relationships with her loved ones and especially with her father.

Her poignant memoirs provide a rich context to the depths and the heights that true forgiveness can reach. So for her it is to forgive and remember, not forgive and forget. Not remember in a grudging and bitter way but in a reflective way that remembers not only the unmerited favour we have all received but also the markers on the road to reconciliation we hold dear.

Robert Bickle, MD

***

Zdenka Slama's first book, *Limping Through Forgiveness,* is a beautiful example of the power of forgiveness to dispel guilt, fear and hatred. Jesus said, *"Follow me."* In doing so we are called to forgive. Forgiveness is the only weapon that can free us from the pain caused by betrayal. Some betrayals are worse than others, and Zdenka experienced the deepest kind of betrayal, inflicted by her father and mother. She takes us through the dark days of a faithless childhood in Czechoslovakia under the influence of Communist ideologies, her escape from a life of fear, her newfound faith, and an outcome that would seem to be impossible—except that nothing is impossible with God.

She shows us that there is really no way to save us from the suffering caused by others until we are saved from ourselves, from our own guilt, fear and hate. There is no freedom from our suffering until we release our oppressors through forgiveness. I recommend this book especially to those who have experienced the pain of abuse by parents and caregivers. It will give you another perspective and a new sense of what freedom can be.

Teresa Marchildon, Chaplain, Correctional Services

Forewords

***

In the world of hurt, pain, and personal rejection that so many people live in, there is a need for honest, gentle, and wise guides to walk beside them. Zdenka Slama is just such a guide. As she courageously walks us through the many dark valleys of her own life, we soon discover that we are actually journeying along a path towards wholeness and healing. *Limping Through Forgiveness* does not offer a quick fix; it offers real hope, refined in the fire of real life, and the freedom that can be found in genuine forgiveness.

Brian D. Cunnington, Professor Emeritus, Counselling Tyndale Seminary

***

What a delight to read the amazing journey of someone I served with for many years in ministry. Being Zdenka's pastor for over 15 years was an honor and privilege. I watched some of these chapters happening but realize from reading her book just how much I didn't know.

I marvel at how God brought the right people at the right time to walk with her. I rejoice in the gracious and persistent way the Father loved His daughter and slowly but surely transformed her bruised and broken heart.

Zdenka, with masterful tenderness, opens the door into our hearts by revealing the struggles experienced in hers. You need to read this story. It will encourage and convict. It will shine light into places needing hope. Be open to what she so masterfully gives and be ready to let the true light of life shine upon you.

Forgiveness isn't easy, but essential if we are to experience the healing grace of God in the everyday reality of our far from perfect lives. What a gift.

Rev. Brent Farquhar

Preface

What you are about to read is a personal account of my struggle with forgiveness. A few names have been changed to protect their anonymity. Although I speak a lot about me, my thoughts, my feelings, and my struggles, I do not want you to think that I am boasting about me and what I was able to do and overcome in my life. Not at all!

The true desire of my heart is that you will read my story as a tribute to the power of God and what He is able to do in us and through us when we come to Him and rest our case before Him. I want you to read my story only as a lower story pointing to the higher story, without which there could never be the lower story, neither yours nor mine. The glory belongs to God! It is He who can bring all of us victoriously through life, no matter how hardened our hearts are, if we will only give Him a chance. There is forgiveness to receive and to give anytime you are ready to turn the page and start a new life. Only be aware that true forgiveness goes deeper than the incomplete "half-baked" forgiveness frequently passed around.

I pray that in reading my story you will increase not only your understanding of God and His gift of forgiveness but also your understanding of yourself and others. Not everything in this book will work for everybody, because God leads each one of us along different paths. The key to victory is to be faithful wherever God leads you.

Forgiveness can be a complicated issue for survivors of domestic violence or anyone living with a batterer, especially believers in Christ.

I suggest consulting a professional experienced in dealing with violence in relationships and familiar with the forgiveness process and boundaries.

"Some situations should never be tolerated, even to keep a marriage together."*

***

The book is divided into four sections based on the stages of forgiveness. In the appendix at the end of the book I have included questions for each stage to help you with your own journey through forgiveness.

***

"Forget the former things; do not dwell on the past. See, I am doing a new thing! Now it springs up; do you not perceive it? I am making a way in the desert and streams in the wasteland." (Isaiah 43:18–19, NIV)

---

* Arterburn, S. *The 7 Minute Marriage Solution.* Brentwood, TN: Worthy Publishing, 2013.

Section A
Admitting

Whatever life holds for you and your family in the coming days, weave the unfailing fabric of God's Word through your heart and mind. It will hold strong, even if the rest of life unravels.

- Gigi Graham Tchividjian

I waited patiently for God to help me; then he listened and heard my cry. He lifted me out of the pit of despair, out from the bog and the mire, and set my feet on a hard, firm path, and steadied me as I walked along. He has given me a new song to sing, of praises to our God. Now many will hear of the glorious things he did for me, and stand in awe before the Lord, and put their trust in him. (Psalm 40:1–3, TLB)

Chapter I

Bitter? Who, Me?

One day, while visiting our friends and staying after supper, our talk turned to our families we grew up in. Suddenly our friend turned to me and said, "You sound bitter."

I was shocked and, to be honest, a little offended. Bitter? *Me?*

He continued, "If you had truly forgiven your parents you wouldn't sound so bitter."

"You don't know what happened, Glenis," I said, trying to reason with both him and myself at the same time.

Glenis didn't let up. "All I said is, you wouldn't sound bitter if you'd forgiven them."

His words made me angry. How dare he! He had not lived through the nightmares I had! He hadn't been there when my dad beat up my mom, when he called her stupid or a slut, when he slapped her face and threw her against a wall. He hadn't been there when Dad yelled and screamed in fury because the meal was not ready on time. How dare he judge me! In the face of all that, how could he even speak about forgiveness? I was considering whether Glenis was even my friend. How could he say I was bitter?

Limping Through Forgiveness

On the way home I asked my husband, "Do I really sound bitter?"

"I don't know about that," was his diplomatic answer, "but if you *have* forgiven them, why are you so defensive when somebody asks about your parents? What happened, happened. Why are you still so angry about it?"

Yes, Peter was right. I did get defensive when somebody mentioned my parents. Why did I feel I had to explain to everyone what happened between us? The conversation etched itself into my memory, and over the next few years I would return to it again and again, remembering my friend's words "You sound bitter." Why had those words pierced me so deeply? Had I still not forgiven them? How did one act when one had truly forgiven? The fact that I preferred not to associate with my parents didn't mean I had not forgiven them, did it? How could anyone understand what had gone on in our home behind the closed door? Who would believe me? Would anyone even care?

After all, my life was pretty good now. God had done a tremendous work in me, changing me from an atheist to a believer. I certainly didn't want to sound like a victim. No, I didn't want to live in my past, but my past continued to follow me like a black cloud threatening to engulf me. I didn't want to go back and rake over old hurts, but I knew I needed to do something about the hold my past seemed to continue to have over me. I just didn't know what.

***

I was seven or eight years old when my parents had one of their many fights. I remember standing underneath a crucifix that hung on one of our walls. It had the figure of a man stretched out on it. I knew he had to be somebody powerful because my grandma told me to come and talk to him whenever I needed help. I loved my grandmother, and I trusted her.

Periodically I would come to the cross on the wall in our bedroom and ask the man hanging on it to please speak sense to my parents and make them stop yelling and hurting each other.

That day I was crying and pleading with him once again. But Dad kept on screaming, and Mom kept trying to calm him down, crying, "Please, stop! Stop for kids' sake! Stop, *please!*" The argument went on and on as I kept praying to the man on the cross to please make my parents stop fighting and screaming at each other. But the man on the cross didn't move, and he didn't come down to talk sense to my parents.

After a while the room grew darker and the noise in the kitchen subsided. As I started to relax in the stillness after the storm, I heard the front door close with a loud bang. I came out of my room fearing the worst and found Mom collapsed on a chair at the kitchen table. "He's left," she said quietly.

This was bad news! It meant that Dad would not show up for a few days, or, if he *did* come home, he would not talk to Mom, and more doors would be banged and things would be thrown. I went back to my room, made a fist with my right hand, and shook it at the crucifix. I was furious with the man that hung on it.

I hissed at him, "You are not! You are *not*! I cannot trust You! Now I have to help myself."

I curled up in the corner of my room, alone with my pain. As far as I could tell there was no one who cared. The teachers in my school were right. There was no God. There was nobody to help me.

***

Soon after that was All Saints' Day. On that day, those who have died are remembered with fresh flowers and burning candles on their graves. Just prior to this holiday, the graves are given what, for most of them, is their once-a-year sprucing up. Weeding and prettifying the graves was my mother's job.

Sometimes she brought along my sister and me. This one particular All Saints' Day, in the evening, my dad and I went to visit my grandmother's grave with flowers and candles. As the candles were lit, Dad and I stood quietly in prayer or memories or both. I noticed that his eyes were red, while I cried uncontrollably. We both shared a deep love for his mother. It seemed like after she died everything had gone from bad to worse. I missed her incredibly.

On the way home I asked Dad what happens to people when they die. "Is there something after death?" I wanted to know.

"No, there is nothing, nothing at all."

"Not another world?"

"No."

"Why do we live then? What is the reason for it? Life makes no sense." I remember being really puzzled and feeling lost.

Dad must have sensed it, because he tried to encourage me. "Since this life is all you have, try to live it as best you can, and when you grow old, as we all must, you will be satisfied with how you lived your life. Try to help people and leave some memory behind. This way you will live forever in their memories."

"And when those people die, then who is going to remember me?" I asked, and I felt this vast, incredible and utter hopelessness. A strange feeling of an enormous void and tremendous emptiness and uselessness of life came over me. In that moment, I really felt that I didn't want to live.

As if Dad had read my thoughts, he said, "You are too little to ask such big questions. Simply live as best you can, because this life is all you have, and you can waste it or make it good. Be a doctor, and you will be able to help many people, and they will love you and remember you. Become the best doctor you can be."

Ever since I could remember, Dad had wanted me to become a doctor. To him that must have been the ultimate in human achievement. I wasn't too sure about being a doctor, though, since I didn't like blood.

"Dad, can a doctor heal by words only?" I asked him.

"What do you mean? How would that work?" he wanted to know.

"I will just touch people and say some words, and they will be healed."

"Nonsense—I have not heard about anybody healing like that. Maybe people heal like this in Africa, but they are not real doctors. Real doctors go to school for many years, have straight As all through, obey their parents and are number one in everything they do."

After a while he added, "People say that there once was a man who healed by words and touch, but I don't know."

Sometimes I wonder if Dad had Jesus on his mind. I never found out.

Chapter 2

The Fight

Out of my parents' many fights two specific ones imprinted themselves on my brain and ruled my life from the backseat. The first one happened when I was in grade 2. My parents quarreled in front of me about how they were fed up with one another. Openly and angrily they discussed a divorce. I didn't even know what that meant. Dad asked me who I preferred to live with. I was doing my homework and pretended not to hear the question. He asked me again, and I knew this time I had to answer.

"Do you really mean what you're saying?" I asked, dreading his answer. "You and Mom don't want to live together, and I have to go and live with either you or Mom?"

"Yes," he said.

I thought about it for a bit. They both looked surprised that I took so long in answering, but I couldn't make up my mind. I loved them both. Finally, I chose Dad, but he didn't like that.

"No. No, you really cannot come and live with me. How would I ever take care of you? I cannot cook like your mom. You will be better off with her."

His words hurt me very much. I couldn't understand why my father would first ask me to choose and then reject me and my choice. I couldn't understand why my parents had to toss me between themselves like some beach ball. How does a child choose between her parents? Mom was hurt and mad at me for choosing Dad over her. "You deceitful little traitor," she spat at me, and this is how she continued to see me for much of my life.

Whenever my sister and I had a squabble or even a little disagreement, I would get a beating because I was "the older one and should have more sense than to argue." Shame, guilt and fear followed me for years to come. Those feelings hung around our apartment and saturated the very air we breathed. Sometimes people who knew me would stop me in a store or on the street and gently inquire why I looked so sad, and the teachers at school would take me aside and ask me if everything was all right. My answer was always the same. "Yes, everything is all right." And indeed, everything was "all right," since I didn't know any different.

***

Shortly after that came the second fight, the nightmare night. I woke up to the sounds of Dad screaming and Mom crying and, once again, begging him not to be so loud or he would awaken the kids. I crawled out of bed and tiptoed into the kitchen. I cracked the door open and saw the tablecloth and plates and cutlery on the floor and Dad hitting Mom in the face.

"No! Don't!" I screamed.

Dad turned around, jumped towards me, grabbed me by my hair and hissed, "If you don't want to end up the same, go to bed *now!*"

I couldn't move and continued to scream. "Please, Daddy, don't. Please, don't!"

"Stop! Stop it now!" Dad barked at me again, but I couldn't stop.

The Fight

He turned to Mom, pulled her by her arms, opened the door of the apartment, pushed her through and closed it behind her. I wanted to go after her, but Dad threatened to kill me if I didn't stop "carrying on." He tore my mom's clothes from the hangers, pulled them out of drawers, dumped them on a sheet on the floor and bundled it up. He opened the door and threw the bundle after Mom, who had not moved.

I don't know how I ended up back in the room with my sister, who was two years younger than me. Although she had missed most of it, she was now wide awake. I sat beside her on the cot, crying. Somehow we both fell asleep and survived the night. It was a night that frightened me to the innermost core of my being.

In the morning Mom was back in the kitchen with a bruised face and arms. "If you had kept quiet yesterday and minded your own business, I wouldn't have ended up like this," she said reproachfully. Suddenly I, not Dad, was the bad guy. She blamed me for what had happened.

I was not allowed to go to school. Dad wrote me a sick note, saying that I had a headache, and warned me not to tell anyone what happened in our home. I wished someone would come and help us, but nobody came. The discrepancy between my way of seeing things and Mom's way of explaining them had me very confused and disturbed me to the point where I started second-guessing myself. What I had seen was an angry Dad physically beating my mom and throwing her out of the apartment. Yet she claimed that none of it would have been so bad had I stayed out of it.

Chapter 3

The Effects of Violence and Abuse

In retrospect, Mom probably denied the reality of what was going on in order to be able to function on a daily basis. In a strange way, while denial "helped" her to continue her miserable existence, it also prevented her seeking healthier ways of living. Mom had no friends and did not confide in her parents, for fear of upsetting them. She started to drink and smoke and use strong headache medication that she sent me to buy.

"Are you here again?" the pharmacist asked. I didn't know what to say, and I blushed.

"Who do you want this for?"

"My mom," I said timidly.

"Tell her she needs to come here herself. We will not sell it to you any longer, because it is a strong medication."

"Did you get it?" my mom asked me when I got home.

I sadly shook my head. "No. The man said you have to go and get it yourself."

"Since when? Is he stupid? Now my headache is even stronger and I have nothing to help me."

She went and lay down and told me and my sister to be quiet. This was not unusual. Mom had frequent migraines, and noise and bright lights, or even daylight, only made it worse. Quiet and dark was the norm in our place. The next day she sent me to another drugstore and after that to another. Here and there I overheard Mom asking her sister or her mother to get the pills for her in the places they lived or worked. With hindsight I now know Mom was addicted. I wonder if she knew herself. It must have been hard for her to face the abuse. It must have been hard to think that she was not loved.

***

Once, when I was eight or nine, I had a very high fever, and I wanted Mom to come sit beside me on the bed. "Mommy, please come and hold my hand. I am afraid."

"There is nothing to be afraid of; it is only a fever. You will be fine." She was sewing something in the corner opposite to my bed and was in a hurry to get it finished. She did not turn to look at me.

After a while I begged again. "Mommy, please come and sit beside me. What if I die?" I was really scared.

"So you die. It would be better if you were dead."

Thinking I had not heard her correctly I asked again, "Mommy, you want me to die?"

"Life would be much easier if you had never been born," she said.

It was then that I started to cry, softly and into the pillow so she would not hear me. After a while she came and knelt beside my bed and asked me to forget what she had said, that she did not know why she had said it, and not to tell Dad.

***

The chaos of our home left me heartbroken and confused, feeling guilty and ashamed much of the time. No matter how hard I tried, I always seemed to do the wrong thing, and Mom would tell me again and again that I should be ashamed for not knowing better. These feelings of anxiety, fear, guilt and shame accompanied me well into my adult years: I would feel anxious when alone and anxious in a crowd of people; I continued to fear my dad and to fear for my mom, my sister and me; I felt ashamed for the yelling and fighting that continued in our home; I felt guilty for Mom's suffering, guilty for being born.

***

"What happens at home stays at home," Dad and Mom used to tell my sister and me. We were constantly reminded never to talk to anyone about our family. We also weren't allowed to have friends in and seldom did anyone come to see our parents. If they came, they didn't stay long.

Dad always found something wrong with every one of Mom's girlfriends and forbade her to see them. He isolated her from any possible support to keep her under his control. Occasionally he would tell her that she was crazy.

"You do not know what you are saying; that is not how it is. You are imagining things. You belong in asylum" was his conclusion when Mom tried to point out stuff he did not like to hear.

I think that all three of us, Mom, my sister and I, feared Dad as much as we loved him. All three of us took a different stance to ward off our fear of Dad and the confusion and uncertainty that was our life. Mom tried to appease him as much as she knew how, becoming very compliant in the process. Occasionally she muttered to herself, "Maybe I am crazy; maybe he is right." I figured that as long as I excelled in school, which made Dad happy, I would be safe. My sister, on the other hand, turned into the family clown and the daredevil troublemaker. Dad liked her daring attitude, and Mom liked her fun-loving personality. Anna was a tomboy, and we even gave her a boy's nickname—Hans (Honza in Czech).

We both tried to stay away from our house as much as possible. I volunteered in many after-school activities, and Mom often commented that if I could sleep at school, I would. My sister, the total opposite of me, had a knack for constantly getting herself into trouble, both in school and after school. Mom said that she was looking for trouble and always found it, or trouble found her. Each one of us relied on different things to manage life as best we could. Later on my sister and I started to drink, and she added smoking too.

Chapter 4

Navigating Life's Stormy Seas

The messages I received throughout my childhood were often contradictory and confusing. Be nice, do well in school, there is no hope for you in the world if you don't learn how to cook, be seen but not heard, of course I love you, I wish you weren't born, I am sacrificing myself for you, you are so selfish, why can't you be more loving like your sister, why don't you smile, stop crying or I'll teach you not to cry, and on and on and on. But mostly the words "You should have never been born" buzzed in my head like an angry swarm of bees.

Dad and Mom continued to live together on and off for a few more years, but things kept escalating from bad to worse. Preoccupied with themselves and their fights, they had no time to get meaningfully involved with us children on a daily basis. Although Dad occasionally took us skiing in the winter and to a cottage during the summer, the trips often became a continuation of their fights. Instead of joyous anticipation, I started dreading the outings. There actually came a time when I wished they would divorce so there would be peace and quiet and I could do my homework.

I also hated having to be a confidante to my mother. I couldn't understand why she had to tell me all her junk; I especially hated her junk about Dad, since there was nothing I could do to help her anyway. I admired Dad for never speaking badly against Mom. When I asked him directly about what was going on, he only said, "You are too young to understand now. When you grow up you will understand the adult business better."

So, with too much information on one hand and not enough on the other, how was I to make sense of life? I learned to suppress my anger and turn off my tears of sadness early in life. Somehow, I thought that the less noise I made, the less visible I would be, and the better the situation would turn out for me. I strived for that invisibility so Mom would think of me as low-maintenance and keep me. When salesclerks commented on how very quiet and obedient I was, she would say proudly, "I don't even know I have two children! She knows better than to upset me—she knows if she doesn't listen she can pack up and go, right?" Mom would look at me and raise her eyebrows. Whenever I couldn't fall asleep I would mentally prepare a list of things to take with me if I ever had to suddenly pack up and go: my schoolbag and my textbooks, some nice clothes, books to read, and my skates.

Since I loved to read, books became my most cherished friends. They offered a better world than the one I lived in, an oasis in the middle of my war zone. They carried me into places of kindness, gentleness and order, where happy parents had happy children and nobody fought. With books I didn't have to second-guess myself. I could be who I was. I didn't have to pretend not to hear and not to see. I was free to think and free to dream.

As I grew older, I added skating, track and field, and downhill skiing to my ways of escape. These activities became my coping skills to control what I could control and to distance myself from what I could not control. Busyness and competitiveness became my two major coping skills—ones that I still have to keep an eye on and watch out for. I used them heavily in the early part of my marriage. When I did not know how to work out a conflict with my husband, I escaped into another part of the house—to read a book or close myself off inside my sewing room or clean like a madwoman—or worked in the garden or took night courses or joined a small group…I did all these things after putting in an eight-hour day at the hospital where I worked as the central supply technician. Work, work, and more work, taking on more than I could handle, trying to fill the void inside me, trying to "earn my keep," trying to be good and make people happy. It didn't work. The feelings of security and significance lasted only as long as the mist that rises early in the morning, stays for a brief moment, and then burns up in the bright, hot sun.

Chapter 5

God Behind the Scenes

My parents eventually divorced. I was fourteen years old and in the hospital after a serious ski accident, when they came to tell me about it.

"So we did it," Mom said.

"Did what?"

"Well, you know what," she said evasively.

"No, I don't. What is going on?" I was curious to know.

"You really don't know? Then ask your dad."

When I asked Dad, he was just as evasive and told me to ask Mom.

"What is happening?" I asked both of them, feeling uneasy and confused.

"We are now divorced!" Mom announced, as if she won a windfall. For her, I think, it was a breakthrough, standing up for herself, perhaps for the first time in who knew how many years.

Once the divorce was finalized, however, another set of difficulties emerged. Life turned out to be economically very difficult for my mother, my sister and me. I used to collect paper and metal and bring it to our town's recycling depot.

Limping Through Forgiveness

Besides getting paid for it and thus contributing to my mom's income, it also helped me get points for my pioneer badges at school and helped the state to curb waste.

Mom felt that the mental, emotional and sometimes physical abuse she suffered at the hands of my father was easier to take than the economic hardship she put herself and us through with the divorce. She blamed herself for the situation and periodically contemplated suicide. Maybe this is where I got my own idea about suicide later on when I was sixteen. It kept me occupied for a few days, but I concluded that "they" would bury me with a lot of hoopla and many fake tears, and nothing would change for anyone. This made me change my mind. I decided to live to see how much worse life could become.

***

I adored my dad, but I loved my mother. She was a gentle person in many ways, and I admired that a lot, but it was Dad who became my role model. He represented the ultimate authority and power, which I believed to be of utmost importance in life. It got him what he wanted, while Mom seemed to be a weakling. I resolved never to put up with what she put up with.

Right up until grade 5, I prided myself in being strong, being able to hold in my tears, and never needing to ask anyone for help. I took to fighting in school, and I really enjoyed beating up the boys. Without realizing it, I was turning into a bully! No teacher ever apprehended me, as I was careful to fight only when they weren't around; and since I only fought with boys, they never complained, probably because they were too ashamed to admit being beaten by a girl.

Years later, while visiting my sister, I asked her about the fights for which she had been not only expelled from school but even made to transfer to one in a different district. She first denied it, but later she remembered that she had been beating up on the boys. She didn't know that I had done the same until I told her. After we exchanged our stories we had a long laugh and agreed that it had been our way of punishing Dad.

***

Shortly after the divorce, Dad took me to visit his mother's sister, my great-aunt, in Vienna. I was amazed at how much she resembled my grandmother and equally amazed at how very different Austria was from Czechoslovakia. I knew from my history lessons that they had once been a unified country, but in my teen years I was shocked by how these two countries were miles apart in ideology and in lifestyle. Never before had I seen stores filled with so many material goods like I did in Vienna. The purses, shoes and clothing, all in beautiful colours and different designs, simply overwhelmed my senses. Wide, clean and orderly boulevards, nice cars driving on the roads, food stores stuffed to overflowing with fresh fruit and flowers, men in white dress shirts, and women smartly dressed and made up. Smiling and relaxed people were everywhere I looked.

Growing up in Czechoslovakia under the influence of socialist and Communist ideologies, I firmly believed that they were the only answer to an ailing humanity and the only key to human happiness. When Dad spoke about countries where you could come and go as you pleased, I could not imagine it, so I grew content with life as I knew it, believing it to be the best kind of life there could be. It was easy to think this way because this was what I had been taught from grade 1, and until now, I had seen nothing to contradict or challenge my beliefs.

But now, in Vienna, my eyes were opened to a different way of life. I sensed a freedom I didn't know existed. I don't know if a person can fully understand what real freedom feels like unless they have also experienced life without it. Freedom is something you cannot touch or see. It needs to be lived, and it needs to be experienced. If you have never known freedom, you will not miss it, but once you are introduced to it, you won't be able to live without it. Just like being in love—it is an indescribable feeling! When I came face to face with the discrepancies between what I learned in school about freedom and what I observed in Austria, I couldn't deny that what we were being taught back home was a lie. I pondered the difference between these two freedoms and became disillusioned with the one that I lived in.

Needless to say, I didn't want to return to Czechoslovakia; unfortunately, I had to or else the government would see it as a defection and punish Mom and Anna (who remained under their power) as a deterrent to others who would attempt to leave the country. All the way home I considered different ways of waking people up to what was behind the barbed wire. I realized I could never go back to life as I had known it up to that point without trying to change it for the better. Hopefully, as a journalist, I dreamed, I would have my chance.

***

A couple of years later, Mom was distressed to find out that Dad was living with a twenty-year-old. Because I had a hard time believing that Dad could live with somebody only slightly older than myself, I offered to go and assess the situation and report back to Mom. I was curious about the woman. What did she look like? Was she the reason Dad had no time for Anna and me anymore? Didn't he know how much it hurt us? I nervously rode the tram to my father's apartment and apprehensively knocked at the door.

Instead of Dad, a beautiful young blonde answered it.

"What are you doing here?" I asked.

"I live here," she said.

"I want to speak with my dad."

"Your dad is not here," she lied. As soon as she said that, I heard Dad asking who was at the door. "Your daughter," she told him.

It felt so creepy and wrong—a stranger having more right to my dad than I did. My father didn't come to the door but asked this woman to let me in. I felt like he didn't care one way or the other, and frankly, I didn't know how to behave. I didn't feel like kissing him when he was kissing this young thing. I didn't want to see how they lived. Suddenly, he too became a stranger to me. I stayed outside and talked to the blonde, asking her questions like what she did for a living and why she lived with an old man like my dad. I wanted to make him appear undesirable to her, but it didn't work. Mind you, he was only about thirty-nine years old at the time and good-looking, as was my mom. The blonde gave the predictable answers: she loved him, he loved her, he provided for her, that sort of thing.

After talking to her for almost half an hour without Dad ever coming to the door, I turned and left. A beautiful young blonde had been chosen over me, and I felt like an outsider. Rejected and unwanted once again…wasn't life strange? Dad had a new woman in his life, and Mom had a new man in her life, but where did I fit? *Life sucks,* I thought, once again considering what the best way to end it would look like. Once again I decided against the idea.

***

It was the Christmas before my high school graduation. An elderly lady, whose husband was a doctor at the local clinic, came to visit us. She brought us some chocolates, cookies and money. As the woman chatted with Mom, one word caught my attention: "God."

I turned to her, full of scorn. "Such an intelligent woman like you [she spoke four languages], believing in God?!"

She became a little uneasy. To believe in God in a Communist country was to ask for trouble, especially if you had a high profile in the community, like her husband did. It would have been easy for me to report her to the authorities. Nobody could be certain about anyone's integrity.

I will never forget her reply. "Well, my mom believes in God, and she tells me that He exists. I love her, and I have no reason to doubt her."

I remembered meeting her mother a couple of times. She was a very old and much wrinkled woman, bedridden for many years. She would hold my hand in her very thin, cold one and tell me that she prayed for me. I felt doubtful but good at the same time.

That night I could not get her daughter's strange testimony about God out of my mind. I opened up the window in the bedroom that I shared with my sister. Moonlight bathed the sleeping town in a strange glow. The snow glistened and cracked in the freezing temperature of the night. The sky was gorgeous, richly and beautifully embroidered with many stars. I thought about God and whispered quietly, "God, if you really exist, please take me out of this country before next Christmas." As an afterthought I added, "Please give me a husband different from my dad."

***

In early spring, after that memorable Christmas visit, I had to go to a journalists' meeting in my hometown. It was about the usual political stuff, and as a starting freelancer for the one of the regional papers, I was asked to write a report about it. This was only a few short months before my graduation. The meeting seemed to finish, and people started to leave, but only some. Fearful of missing something important, I asked a young man if the meeting had really ended.

"Are you a member of the Communist Party?" he replied.

"No," I answered honestly, since I was only nominated for the Communist Party but not yet a member.

"Stay then, but do not tell anyone about this," he cautioned. His answer made me very curious and somewhat frightened.

Soon new people started to arrive, and another meeting began shortly. There was some talk about unrest in different parts of Czechoslovakia and how people who opposed the Communist regime were jailed and some were never heard of again. There was talk about things not being right in the country and about an underground movement growing daily. My head was spinning. Was this for real? Were these things really happening? Was I being given the privilege of witnessing the birth of a revolution? Brought up to distrust everyone and everything, I wondered if this could be a trap to test me, since I had been nominated for membership in the Communist Party. I decided to leave.

Back at the office, I scribbled a few notes and added some of the ideas from the second meeting in the form of questions. I do not remember them exactly, but they seemed innocent enough to me, questions such as "Is everything we see truly what is? Are there things that could be improved? How can they be improved? How could our country be made better for the people?" I laid the report on my boss's desk shortly before midnight.

Early in the morning my boss called me on the phone and woke me up. He told me in no uncertain terms to get to his office instantly. Totally surprised, I dressed and went to see him, hoping to be back at school for eight.

When I arrived, he looked both ways down the corridor, and then he sat me down close to his desk and whispered. "Do you want to destroy your future and be locked up for the rest of your life? What is going on with you? Are you in love or something? Where is your head? How can you be so reckless?"

Stunned by his strange questioning, I couldn't think of how to answer, and I shrugged my shoulders in confusion.

"You are overworked and stressed. You need rest," he decided, and he offered me the use of his cottage so I could relax before final exams and graduation.

When I politely declined his offer, he took the article I had written and burned it in front of me in the ashtray. He said he would not turn me in because I was a promising young journalist with my whole life in front of me and that it would be a pity to forfeit my future in such a stupid way. I dutifully thanked him and went to school.

This was, as they say, "the straw that broke the camel's back." I was face to face with the reality that unless I was willing to co-operate politically, to toe the line of lies and hypocrisy, I would have no chance at a career. I thought long and hard. If I was not allowed to speak the truth, why be a journalist? What was the point? Why stay in a country where I was forbidden to speak about and comment on the reality around me?

***

It was around this time that Mom became friends with a high-ranking secret-police officer. He told her that the police were waiting to take Dad to prison. I knew Dad didn't have a regular job but travelled door-to-door, enlarging and colour-tinting family photos. In the days of black-and-white photographs this was an unusual novelty, and people were willing to pay for it. It was also classified as "illegal moneymaking," because private business was not allowed unless the government had given permission, and Dad wasn't the kind of man to ask for it.

On one of Dad's rare visits during this time period, Mom told him about the impending arrest, and they talked seriously about leaving the country. Neither my parents nor my sister wanted to leave, but Dad knew about the prison conditions and was convinced he would not survive a term. We began planning our escape.

Chapter 6

The Escape

Mom and I easily obtained passports and visas to travel legally to Austria for a holiday, thanks to her friendship with the secret service officer. Dad and Anna didn't apply, knowing they would not get them. It was a routine procedure at the time that if one or two members of a family travelled to the West, the other members had to stay behind to guarantee their return, party members in good standing excepted. Since it was relatively easy to obtain a three-day permit to Hungary, a decision was made that Mom and I would go to Austria and Dad and Anna to Hungary. Once in Hungary they would cross the border illegally into Yugoslavia and then again illegally into Austria, because the three-day permit wouldn't allow them to go anywhere else except Hungary. Mom and Dad established a signal by phone if the crossing over into Yugoslavia was successful. Once we got the signal, Mom and I would have to move quickly through our part of the escape plan.

The final preparations were completed, and Dad and Anna left by nightfall. Mom and I hardly slept at all. At daybreak,

Limping Through Forgiveness

I asked her to go for a walk, perhaps our last walk ever through the city. Mom declined, saying that she wouldn't be able to stop her tears if she saw people she knew, and then they would wonder what was going on. So I went by myself. On the way back I bought a salad and some sweets, but Mom didn't touch any of it, saying she didn't feel well. And so, having packed everything we would be taking, we waited all day by the phone for the signal, our nerves strung tight.

The signal came late that night—two rings, hang up, and then immediately call back with a password. As soon as the phone rang for the second time, Mom grabbed it and held her breath as she listened for the password. It was given, and she placed the phone back in its cradle with trembling hands. "They did it," she breathed out. "They are in Yugoslavia." Then she put her hands to her forehead, headed for the bathroom and was violently sick, vomiting and crying at the same time.

The train to Vienna was leaving at midnight, and we had to make sure we caught it or otherwise risk that the police would come knocking on our door in the morning. In those final, frenzied moments, with suitcases and train tickets in our hands, Mom suddenly became frozen with fear, and she didn't want to leave. She was having a hard time severing herself from the only place that had provided her with what little safety and security she had in her life. Trying to keep her calm, I called the taxi and collected our belongings. For the last time, I looked around at the pictures and the books I had loved and was now leaving behind forever. Then I locked up our flat and hurried us down the stairs. "Mom, the taxi is here. We need to go—*now!*" Finally, with our luggage in the cab and Mom shaking and white as a sheet, we were off to the train station.

We had barely cleared the gate when the train came in at full speed. We boarded quickly and found our seats, but we couldn't relax. The biggest challenge was still ahead of us—

the Austrian border. Even though we had the visa stamped in our passports, it didn't guarantee anything. Both Mom and I worried separately and silently, never giving voice to our worries: had Dad and Anna made it to Austria or had they been turned around and sent back home? What if they had already been caught and now the guards were waiting for us? We simply had no way of knowing.

The train started to slow down—we were approaching the Austrian border. We waited there for over an hour as the guards' German shepherds ran wild, sniffing all around and under our car. The car stood by itself, on a side rail, disconnected from the engine. It seemed that time had stopped. With every minute of waiting, my fears increased considerably.

Finally, they connected our car to another engine, and we started to move slowly across no-man's-land into Austria. I was elated—we had made it through! But I was also deeply saddened by the prospect of never seeing my grandparents or my best friend, Mila, again. None of them had any clue that we were going away and never coming back: in order not to raise any suspicions, we didn't say goodbye to anyone.

***

As the train approached Vienna, we finally allowed ourselves to relax. We had made it! We were tired, and Mom was still pale but felt much better. Although I was only eighteen years old and fresh out of high school, I had the responsibility of taking care of us, because I was the only one who spoke German.

We had hoped to stay with my cousin at his flat in Vienna, but out of the need for secrecy we hadn't been able to let him know ahead of time that we were coming. Our hopes were dashed when he refused to help us.

"I don't understand," he said. "Didn't you have a good life at home? Why are you running away?" He scratched his chin. "I don't want the police at my door. No, you can't stay here.

You have to move on. I can't help you. You should have thought things through before you did this." The fear of imagined punishment prevented him from helping us.

Now we had another problem—the little money we were allowed to exchange was to be for food only. We had nothing left for sleeping accommodations. Not knowing when we would be able to get more money or when and how we would meet Dad and Anna, we were forced to ration what little we had. I tried selling the gifts of Czech crystal we had brought for our relatives, but few people were interested. Somehow I did manage to peddle what we brought in: a vase, an ashtray, and a necklace and earrings, and these got us a few nights' accommodation. During the day we rested in churches, appreciating their coolness and protection from the sun. I prayed that we would soon meet Dad and Anna and that Mom would be happy.

Finally, on Wednesday or Thursday, we had run out of money. I knew we couldn't wait any longer, so I went to the police station and filed a missing persons report. Within half a day Dad and Anna were located, and a good thing too! The officer told us that if we hadn't inquired about them when we did, they would have been shipped back to Czechoslovakia the very next day because they had no passports and Austria had no way of learning their identity. I was very glad and proud of myself for going to the police station when I did, despite Mom's fear of contacting any sort of police and her strong discouragement of it.

The reunion with Dad and Anna was like the promise of a new dawn. But that is all it was. Within a short time of being reunited, the old behavioural patterns quickly re-established themselves. The thing that every one of us three women hoped never to see again happened. Dad picked up his irresponsible behaviour from where he had left off, and Mom resurrected hers—it was the insanity cycle replaying itself all over again.

The Escape

***

We were sent to Traiskirchen, the only refugee camp in Austria at that time. We were housed in barracks together as a family. Within a week my sister and I had found jobs in the kitchen of the hospital in Baden. We were only temporary workers, so when the staff returned from their summer holidays, we were searching for jobs once again. This time, I secured work as a Czech-, Russian- and German-speaking translator in a little shop on Maria-Hilfer Strasse, the most beautiful boulevard in the city of Vienna, one of the main tourist attractions. We hoped we could make our home in Vienna, but it wasn't meant to be.

After a few months, we were given three countries to choose from for our new home: Australia, Canada or South Africa. We picked Canada, and so it happened that I did, indeed, celebrate Christmas far away from Czechoslovakia. God had answered my prayer, long after I had forgotten that I had prayed it.

***

So many miles from my town, so many miles from my grandpa
It's Christmastime here just as it is over there
How are you grandpa...it's been a long time...
I still feel the heat of the summer night when we left
Without saying a word to anyone
I am so sorry, Grandpa, please don't die yet
I wish to see you and hold your hand
One more time

***

After coming to Canada we were in for a culture shock. The architecture, the speed of life, having no friends, hearing only a foreign language all day—all this contributed to our feelings of deep loss and loneliness. I was able to relax and to keep going only when I drank alcohol. Often my thoughts would run along the same course: I had left for freedom, yet here, in the land of plenty and freedom, I didn't *feel* free. Why? Why wasn't I satisfied? What was missing? I was not able to put my finger on "it." After a while I thought that marriage would fix "it."

My husband and I met a year after my family's arrival in Canada. Peter didn't curse, he had a job and a car, and he even said he went to church! I had never expected that anyone still did such an old-fashioned thing like going to church. He was different from all the other young men I had gone out with before. His willingness to talk and listen to me and to respect me endeared him to me. He asked me to marry him, and I agreed, but I told him plain and square, "If you ever lay a hand on me or call me names, I will be out of here and I won't be coming back. I need you to respect me." We promised to respect each other.

The Sunday after we were married my husband started to get ready for church. I reminded him that we had been there only a few days ago to get married. It did not go over well. We quarreled.

I declared, "If I knew you were such a fanatic I would not have married you!"

"If you told me what you are telling me now, I would not have married you either!" Peter answered coldly.

"Don't tell me that you also believe or even read the Bible!" I spat out.

"So what is that to you?"

"If we have any children I suppose you will want to take them to church too?" I retorted.

"If—and that's a big *if*—if we have any children, I will take them to church. If you are still here, you can stay home."

I had never seen him so angry. Face red, forehead wrinkled, eyes in narrow slits, Peter meant business. He continued getting dressed. Against my will I started to get ready too. It might have been the training I received at home, instantly jumping in obedience whenever Dad raised his voice. It might have been the fear of divorce after only one week of marriage. Whatever it was, I began learning the hard way that respect is a two-way street.

***

A few days after we were married I started a dental assistant course, two evenings a week for one year. During the day I worked for a dentist on Spadina Avenue in Toronto. My days were filled with learning new concepts and increasing my English vocabulary, not only with words like "dentures," "root canal" and "extraction," but also "flour" and "roast beef" and "washing detergents."

Amidst the business of living I became pregnant. "Perhaps this baby will make me happy," I hoped. But no such luck. Neither the marriage nor furthering my education nor the birth of our beautiful baby girl the following summer brought me the happiness I hoped for. Rather, I discovered I only had a new set of troubles. What did I want? What was I looking for?

What was missing? I was about to find out.

Chapter 7

Freedom

After our wedding, Peter kept dragging me to church, and our pastor's wife, Ruth, kept inviting me to join this or that Bible study or this or that activity. After some months of politely but firmly declining and Ruth politely persisting, I grew furious. I wanted to have nothing to do with religion, or God, for that matter. Why wouldn't she leave me alone?!

One day I became so fed up that I decided to take Ruth up on one of her offers, merely to be able to get her off my back. Annoyed by her nice persistence, which I had not experienced before, I agreed to go to the Salvation Army with her for a series of worship and praise meetings taking place shortly before Easter in downtown Toronto. The meetings were to run for three consecutive nights. My plan was to go the first night only, "show my face," and then leave. Peter was driving me there with our soon to be two-year-old in the car.

"Why don't you drive around the block?" I told Peter. "I'll be out as soon as I can, perhaps ten, fifteen minutes, max.

I want Ruth to see me there so she will stop bothering me and asking me out. I'll meet you at the front door."

However, when I entered the room Ruth saw me, came over and led me to the seats she had saved for us at the front. Right from the beginning the speaker caught my attention. I don't remember everything he talked about, but I do remember one thing he said: "I was in sales before I became a minister. The pay was good, but working for God pays better wages. Not more, but better." He admitted to needing to have two jobs now to support his family. It puzzled me. How could that be? I wondered how anyone could call himself better off when he had to work at two jobs to have what only one job supplied before. *What a strange philosophy,* I thought. *Is this guy for real? Making less money makes him happier?* The whole thing floored me.

Half an hour later my husband, with our two-year-old daughter in his arms, came up, furious.

"How much longer are you planning to stay?" he asked with lightning in his eyes. "It is cold outside, and we are freezing. I went around the block four times, and you didn't come out. Did you forget I am driving around with a baby and no heater in the car? Besides, she should be in bed—it is past her bedtime."

Ruth overheard his scolding and offered to take me home. I was able to stay for the rest of the evening and satisfy my curiosity. It left me deep in thought, and I didn't want to miss the next two nights. Unbeknown to me, God had started His awesome work in my heart.

After the second evening, Ruth asked me, "Will you come again tomorrow?"

"For sure. I do not want to miss it," I said. She looked pleased and smiled and said something about a special night.

On the third day I woke up with a severe stomach pain and cramps. Add to it a sore throat and a terrible headache, and you might understand why I didn't want to go anywhere. It surprised me because I hadn't felt anything coming on the day before. I didn't remember ever having a headache before. When Ruth called me at lunchtime to find out when to pick me up, I told her very reluctantly that I would not be coming.

"I am as sick as a dog," I told her.

"I don't understand. You felt perfectly well last night," she commented.

"I know, but that was yesterday, and today is today."

"It sounds like the devil doesn't want you to come tonight because he knows what a special night it will be."

"What?!" Stunned, I held the receiver away from my ear, looking at it in disbelief and contemplating hanging up rather than listening to some old-fashioned tales about the devil. Was this woman serious? Believing in a devil and talking about him as if he was real?

"Nina," Ruth's concerned voice cut into my daze. "Are you there; do you hear me?"

"Yes," I answered, dumbfounded. "Ruth, you believe in the devil?"

"No, Nina, I do not believe in the devil. I believe in *God,* who says that there is a devil. The Bible writes about the spirit world around us. Our eyes cannot see it, but it is just as real as the world we live in."

This was a completely new concept to me…but what if Ruth was right? Suddenly I became enraged at the devil for wanting to manipulate me.

"OK," I said. "If what you say is true, then pick me up and I will come with you again tonight."

As soon as I hung up the receiver, I realized that the pain in my stomach was gone and I could walk upright. I was amazed and wondered if there might be some truth to what Ruth was saying. By the time she picked me up, I no longer had a headache, but my throat felt scratchy and I was unable to speak. Out of nowhere I had developed laryngitis.

We drove without speaking and took our usual place at the front. I could only smile, gesture and listen. Midway through the evening there was a refreshment break, and as we went to get our cup of coffee and cookies, I started to tell Ruth how very interesting the evening was and that I actually understood more than I had the first two nights. She looked at me, astonished. "Nina, your voice is back!"

The recognition of that one simple fact startled me. How could that be? The strange and inexplicable things that had been happening to me all day perplexed me.

Over the remainder of the evening the speaker talked about Jesus being the Son of God. He said words I had never heard before, words that cut straight through me into the very marrow of my bones: *"For God so loved the world that he gave his one and only Son, that whoever believes in him shall not perish but have eternal life"* (John 3:16).

I elbowed Ruth. "Is it true, that Jesus was the Son of God?"

"He *is* the Son of God," Ruth corrected me.

"If He died, how can He still live?" The concept made no sense to me. Could I really believe that He loves me? Was it true that Jesus suffered and died for me? I wanted to know. I needed to know. Hundreds of questions were popping into my mind. All at once, a new and unknown world opened its doors and beckoned me.

"Yes, Nina, He loves you, and He loves me, and He loves all the people."

"What must I do for Him to love me so?"

"You don't have to do anything. Just tell Him you are sorry for the things you have done that were not right. Thank Him for loving you much and dying on the cross for you."

"But I haven't done anything wrong—I am a good person," I protested.

The whole thing was overwhelming to me. I was having a hard time digesting and believing that God loved me without expecting anything in return, only that I believe Him. I also couldn't come up with any "sin," as Ruth called it. I honestly thought I was perfect.

After a while Ruth interrupted my thoughts and asked me if there was anything else I wanted to know and, if not, if I would like to ask Jesus to be my Saviour. Somehow, I was not able to give her a straightforward yes or no. Something held me back.

Suspiciously, I asked, "Are you sure that somebody will not come to me tomorrow and want some money?"

"For what?" asked Ruth.

"Well, you said that God is giving me His love for free, but I know that nothing is for free. When and how much will I have to pay?" I was lost in a sea of ideas that were foreign to me.

Ruth was patient. "When you come to God, He takes all the things that you did that weren't good, like lying, cheating, and gossiping about people, and forgives them. It is like wiping a page clean from the writing that you do not agree with anymore and giving you back a clean page to write on."

"Yes, I understand that, but what do I have to do in return?" was my deepest concern that I wasn't able to let go.

"Nothing; just love Him back, pray, and read the Bible to understand Him more and know Him better. It is like a marriage. When you married Peter, you didn't know him very well, did you? But as you live and communicate with him daily, you get to know him better, don't you?"

"Yes," I answered. I wondered if entering a relationship with God is really like entering a marriage. Is He honestly interested in me? Is it possible that there really is such a love?

As if Ruth read my thoughts, she said, "Nina, God loves us more than we can ever imagine."

Wow! The simplicity of it made no sense to me at all, and I kept expecting to come up against some hidden traps. I did not realize at the time that, if there are any traps, they are of our own making. They exist because of what our own minds conjure up, because of how we perceive and interpret things based on the experiences of our past.

I became caught up in the idea that by coming to Jesus my life would suddenly become a piece of cake. I'd have obedient, well-behaved children, a wonderful marriage, good health, prosperity and success. I, I, I...me, me, and me. I thought that Jesus died for me so that I could have not only everlasting life but mainly an easy life while I was still living! It was on this note that I said yes to God's love—yes to what He would do for me, rather than for who He was. At that point, for me God was something like an insurance policy, a "just-in-case." I became a believer only because I figured I had nothing to lose. God's promise was for protection, peace and security—things I longed for deeply.

For a long time I was a nominal believer without knowing it. I would occasionally still drink to get high, but as God's Spirit began to work in me, the drinking slowly started to bother me. I was troubled that I found release in alcohol rather than in God, and I also sensed that if I kept it up I might turn into an alcoholic. One day I got on my knees and pleaded with God to remove any desire for liquor, and I promised to not touch it. As I held a full glass in my hand, the urge to drink it was gone. Immediately I disposed of it in the toilet. After that, whenever the memory of the taste for the alcohol presented itself, I said to myself, "I am not drinking that stuff; I will not drink it," and I found something else to occupy my hands and my mind.

Freedom

***

I am standing at the crossroads today
And in sharp contrast to yesterday
I know where I want to go
But something pulls me back
To the shine of diamonds and cigarettes' smoke
Back to the crowds of people
Where body tangled with the body
Screams in the evaporation of alcohol
O God, please help me win this fight
I wish to belong to You alone
My hands and feet and mouth be at Your service day and night
No king or queen or president nor any other man
But You alone, my Lord, lead the way

Chapter 8

A Separation

On one particularly humid summer day in the beginning of August, my sister called me from the Pearson International Airport in Toronto. She said she was flying with her children to visit our parents, who after living in Canada for about ten years had moved back to Austria. They said they could never adjust to the fast-paced North American lifestyle. My sister asked me to let them know, when they called, that her flight had been delayed and she would be arriving late. She didn't say anything more or answer any of my questions, saying she was already late and the last one to board the plane.

Later that night Dad called.

"Hello?"

"Is that you, Zdenka?"

"Yes, Dad, it's me. How are you?"

"I am calling to see if you spoke with your sister."

"Yes, she said to tell you that the flight was delayed and she will be late landing."

"Is that all? Has she said anything else?"

"No, why?"

"She didn't say anything else?"

"No, Dad. Why do you keep asking me that? Is something wrong?"

"She didn't tell you she is leaving her husband and coming to live with us?"

"What?! With the kids?"

"That's right."

"It doesn't sound right." I was fumbling for words. "Something is not right."

"What is not right? He beats her, doesn't take care of the kids—what do you mean, it is not right?" Dad was getting louder.

"Something is not right. This is the first time I have heard about Brian beating her. She's never said anything to me."

"Why should she? She was ashamed of it." Dad was calming down.

"Why didn't you tell me?" I wanted to know.

"Ask your mother why she didn't tell you."

I realized what was bothering me about the situation. "Dad, it is not right taking the kids and leaving for another country. How will Brian get to see his kids?"

"What do you suggest your sister is supposed to do?" Dad was getting angry again.

"I don't know, but perhaps she can move to BC or another province but stay within Canada. The kids need their dad."

Dad took time before he spoke. "He would find her in Canada. She is afraid of him."

"Well, I know that Eva is crazy about her father. When I spoke with the kids this past summer, they had just returned from visiting you and Mom, and they both were very happy to be back in Toronto with their dad."

"You don't know what you are talking about. If you don't agree with what's happening, you are not my daughter!"

Nobody had ever disagreed with or stood up to Dad and won. I took a deep breath and swallowed my tears. "Dad, remember, you said it, not me."

Bang! The phone went dead, and pain came in like a flood. It stayed with me for a long time. I felt definitely, absolutely and totally abandoned by the father I adored.

This was the third time he had rejected me: the first time because he felt he couldn't take care of me because I was too young; the second time because of the "Blonde"; this third time because I did not share his opinion! The latest rejection was the most painful because it felt so final. Despite doing what I thought was right, I felt like a bad person for disagreeing with Dad. The insecurity and fear from my younger years returned full force, as did memories of Mom calling me selfish and criticizing me for not being the daughter she expected. Dad once said that anyone who disagreed with him became his enemy. At that time I had asked if this also held true for his children. "Yes," he'd said. "Even if my own children don't agree with me, I will have nothing to do with them; they will no longer be mine. At that moment they will become my enemies."

I wept hard and bitter tears. When I was finished, something in me broke. Based on the interpretation of my painful emotions from the past, I rationalized that the relationship between my parents and me was totally and absolutely over.

I closed the door on my parents, Anna, and the whole affair. I busied myself with my own husband, our children, and my work. Knowing how my parents were, I had a hard time believing the things they had told me, even the story about my sister's abuse. However, as a Christian, I knew I needed to forgive this hurt also and so I tried. I was still hurt and angry. My self-esteem, trust, and pride were badly shaken. I decided to distance myself from all three because I didn't know how to communicate what bothered me. Somewhere I've read that when our ability to love is less than our ability to judge, we irresponsibly withdraw. This was certainly what I was doing at this point in my life. However, God was going to use that distance to work inner healing and to mature me, but it would be many years before I could see it from this point of view.

My sister's husband, Brian, called soon after and asked to speak with my sister and the children, thinking they were with us. I told him they had left him and were in Europe. He immediately drove over to our house and told us his side of the story. In his version of events Brian was, of course, blameless, admitting to "occasional" verbal fights but nothing more. Having lived with my parents' verbal abuse and watching my mom put up with it for so many years, I didn't consider "occasional" verbal fights reason enough to leave a marriage. It never occurred to me that they might be symptoms of deeper trouble or, worse, that Brian wasn't telling me the whole truth. At that time I didn't understand how skillfully abusers hide their behaviours and manipulate both their victims and the truth.

Brian's parents backed up his story and appeared sincerely concerned for their grandchildren and my sister, and I came to the conclusion that Anna and my parents had made an irresponsible decision in breaking up her family. Having grown up as I did, I had a hard time discerning what was true and what was not, and I found it easier to believe a stranger than the parents I had lived with most of my life. I took Brian's side and separated myself from my family.

Section B
Becoming

The truth never becomes clear as long as we assume that each one of us, individually, is the center of the universe.

Thomas Merton

As the Scriptures say, *"If anyone is going to boast, let him boast about what the Lord has done and not about himself"* (2 Corinthians 10:17, TLB).

Chapter 9

Learning to Forgive—
Learning to Love

What does a person do with stored-up anger and disappointment? I tried to control it the best way I knew how. I was nice around strangers, but I would often react in anger towards people closest to me and the most vulnerable—my children. "What's wrong with you? How many times do I have to tell you to put away your clothes? Can't you do anything right?" On and on I criticized them, and my husband too, in a misguided attempt to raise a perfect family, one that would be spared the chaos that I had experienced in mine. The more I tried to control people, the worse my relationships with them became. Over the years I found it easier to withdraw than to try to make myself understood or to understand others.

I had no idea it was possible to dialogue with people in a civil manner—it was not something my parents had modeled for me. Because of this, my husband and I had many rough patches throughout our marriage, the worst being between the 15th and 20th years, when our intimacy was at its lowest and our emotional distance at its greatest. I became consumed with making him understand how I felt, but I could never seem to find the words to express myself.

I remember one day in particular when we went for a drive with the sole purpose of talking together. As usual, a million thoughts were running through my head, but I was silent and tense, overwhelmed with the effort of trying to communicate them sensibly. All I could think of was that it felt like having a herd of cows inside me, each one trying to squeeze out through the narrow gate of my mouth at the same time.

"What was it you wanted to talk about?" Peter asked first.

"There are so many things, I don't know where to start," I answered miserably.

"Just start anywhere," he encouraged.

"Yes, I know. I'm trying, but…I…I can't."

"I'm your husband, and I love you. Do you trust me?"

"Yes," I said, but the truth was that I wasn't sure what trust looked like or how to surrender to it when it showed up.

I sat beside my husband in the car, hoping and praying for a miracle to release the torrent of words and thoughts bursting inside, but it never happened, and after an awkward and painful silence I gave up and mumbled, "Maybe we can talk another time." Frustrated with myself and with him, I ended a conversation that didn't happen, and life continued on, like laundry in the dryer—'round and 'round and 'round…

It was Albert Einstein who gave us a perfect definition of insanity: "Insanity is doing the same thing over and over again and expecting different results." It pretty much described my life. Not knowing how to behave or how relate to people other than the way I had watched growing up, I chose to disconnect and withdraw rather than trying to decipher what was, to me, a complex and foreign language. Then the thing I had desperately tried to control and especially prevent from happening happened: our marriage started to implode.

Without speaking the things that really mattered, it seemed like there was something missing. And there was. What was missing was a meaningful conversation about something more than the work around the house or outside the house, kids at school and their activities after school, or what was for dinner. Sadly, we both fell into the rut of being married. Neither one of us was good at communicating, except for the bare necessities of life. I became depressed. With every fibre of my being I had wanted to be different from my parents. And yet, in many ways I behaved just like them—aggressive like Dad or passive like Mom, depending on the situation.

When I married my husband, our relationship was the polar opposite from the chaotic one my parents had. Unfortunately, although I enjoyed the peace and respect between us, I didn't know how to live without the chaos or ensuing anxiety. I had no knowledge or words to express how I felt and what I felt. For years I actually deliberately introduced and recreated anxiety in situations in order to "feel in control." When my husband was late returning home from work, I would imagine him dead or in the hospital with a heart attack or in bed with somebody else or walking the streets aimlessly because he had lost his job. I imagined the situation so realistically that tears would start flowing! When he finally arrived home, I would give him a tongue-lashing. We would argue and yell, and I would be strangely comforted—this was a familiar territory, and I knew every inch of it.

In the fall of 1989, November 9th, the Berlin Wall had been torn down. We had decided to go to Czechoslovakia the following summer with our children. We had planned to visit family and friends we had not seen in more than twenty years. I wondered if I should include a visit to my parents, and I prayed God would show me. Within days I found a postcard my mom had sent me a few months after Dad had hung up on me. In it she wished me a happy birthday and told me that they loved me. I had never answered it. Rereading it after ten years of silence, I hardened my heart and gave in to fear and self-protection once more. Not wanting to be rejected yet again, and not wanting our children to be exposed to the abusive environment I had grown up in, I disregarded the power, love, mercy and grace of the risen Christ and decided against visiting my parents. In my spirit I knew something wasn't right, but I refused to consider that perhaps the postcard had been God's prompting and I was choosing to disobey Him. Had I looked deeply into my heart I would have known my feelings for what they were: fear, anger, injured pride, remorse and resentment—all pointing to an unfinished, "half-baked" forgiveness. Somehow, in choosing to wrest control from God rather than trusting Him, my need for it grew exponentially.

***

Around this time a friend invited me to a study group that was working through a book called *The Twelve Steps: A Spiritual Journey*. Through a slow and painful process I started to see myself and the situation with my parents differently. I learned to identify and recognize various elements of abuse in my life and to call them what they were.

The physical abuse was fairly straightforward and self-evident, as I remembered the beatings and hair pulling and the kneeling on hard peas or on a scrub brush made from rye stalks. It was harder to admit the sexual abuse, such as the degrading words about women's genitals and the pornographic pictures that were also part of Dad's photographic business. However, by far the most difficult for me to recognize and finally admit was the emotional abuse. It was especially hard because so much of it came from Mom. Her criticism and blaming of me had convinced me that I was always at fault no matter what. I was plagued by chronic guilt and became a people pleaser, always needing to earn approval and praise in order to have any worth. The only thing that kept me going through this study and overwhelming time of self-examination was my daily prayer to God for strength to obey Him and to do what was right, no matter the cost.

The self-examination helped me to see God, others and me more clearly. The first three steps in the study are about surrendering and finding peace with God. Going through them felt like I was standing at the edge of the universe and seeing for the first time the enormous vastness and glory of God. I sneaked a peek at God's magnitude and grandeur I had never experienced before, and I was awed. It gave me the strength to face myself as I am and to view others through a different lens. The program was also the beginning of change for our marriage.

***

Four months later the group was finished, and it was time for me to take the next step. In order to move forward I needed to let go of the past, the things I couldn't change, and embrace responsibility for what I could change—my choices. Peter didn't like some of the changes taking place, and I wasn't sure whether it was worth the hassle. We both had to learn to dance to a different beat and to sing a different song. At times we danced like two tone-deaf people.

At times our marriage resembled a small boat all by itself in a stormy sea. Because my need to speak and be heard and understood meant so much to me, I continued to fight for what I believed would rejuvenate our stale marriage. Sometimes only our love for each other held us together.

As to my parents, I had finally concluded that they were not right in what they did, but I was an adult now. Not speaking to them for so many years suddenly seemed silly. However, five more years went by before I finally mustered enough courage to try to reconnect.

I made a surprise visit. Upon arrival, I waited at the door for a long time before it slowly opened.

Mom stood there rigidly like a soldier at attention. I hugged her, but there was no response on her part. Only wide open eyes, as if she couldn't recognize me. I was deeply hurt. Then Dad hugged me and cried.

The three of us went upstairs, and Mom started to show me pictures of my sister in Germany, telling me how well she was doing. Now and then she would look at me in a strange way, and our conversation went something like this:

"Who are you?"

"I'm your daughter, Mom," I answered, feeling hurt and confused.

"I know you are my daughter, and sometimes you look like her, but other times you don't. She was younger—you are older."

"Mom, it's been fifteen years—you have changed too."
"And how are my little ones—how many children do you have?"

"Two, Mom, remember?"

"Tell me their names again—it has been such a long time."

"Claudia and Craig."

"Are they in school now? Why aren't they here?"

"Mom, they're both at university. They're not little kids anymore."

"How the time flies," she said flatly, and I was sad.

Then she told me she heard voices and had even spoken with her dead mother-in-law. I was disturbed and suspected some sort of mental illness. The possibility of Alzheimer's didn't even enter my mind.

"What's going on with Mom?" I asked Dad later.

"I don't know. She doesn't cook or clean anymore. Now I have to do it," he said indignantly.

***

Later, with both of my parents present, I asked them to forgive me, just as I had forgiven them. I was hoping to impress them with my humility—after all, they had caused the break in our relationship, not I.

"What did you say? Just as *you've* forgiven us?!" They were amazed by my words, but not in the way I had hoped for.

"Yes, can you please forgive me just as I have forgiven you?" I repeated, suddenly unsure of myself, a powerless child again, afraid of being hit.

"Who do you think you are talking to? What did we do that you needed to forgive us?!"

Supporting themselves with the palms on the table, they were angrily glaring at me. Enraged and deeply offended by my words, they could not see that they had done anything wrong.

I started to explain. "Dad, you hung up on me and told me I wasn't your daughter."

He didn't let me finish. "What are you talking about? I don't remember any such thing! It's all in your head!"

Was he trying to play the same mind games with me that he used with Mom, or did he really not remember?

He continued, "Don't talk to me this way. My ulcers are starting to act up. You're making me sick!"

The discussion did little to reconcile our stubborn hearts, which were all looking to dish out blame rather than genuinely wanting to forgive.

Needless to say, the rest of the visit didn't go well. There was still too much self-righteousness in me, which prevented me from fully forgiving.

A few more years passed by. I sent token communications—birthday cards and letters—but there was no response. I became even more bitter and resentful. The rejection hurt. I struggled with my feelings, and I wondered if God was punishing me.

***

The years of disconnection from my parents, in which I harboured anger and bitterness towards them, loomed behind me as the darkest years of my life. They were also casting a shadow on my present relationships. I struggled in almost all of them. I called myself a Christian, prayed, read the Bible, went to Bible studies and even led several small groups. However, self-pity kept me in a victim mode. I blamed others for their faults without fully accepting responsibility for my own. In rationalizing the motives behind my behaviour and covering up my anger so that I "looked" like a saint, I was playing the devil's game.

Again my heart was telling me that something was not adding up, but I had neither the skills nor the tools to explore and correct it. I felt powerless and defeated. I spoke to at least three different pastors and a couple of different speakers about the situation between my parents and me, and they all agreed that I had done nothing wrong and that, as long as I had forgiven my parents, I could stand before God with a clear conscience. But they had no skills to see into the depths of my soul, and I was still left looking for peace.

Shortly after this visit to my parents, I lost my job due to the amalgamation and restructuring of two local hospitals. I'd been working as a technician there for fifteen years and had planned to retire there. Now it was obvious that this wasn't going to happen. To say that the loss of my job was a shock would be an understatement. I went into a deep situational depression for three solid days. I didn't eat, shower, comb my hair, clean or cook—I just stayed in bed.

On the fourth day my husband said, "If I come home and find you still in bed, unwashed and crying, I am taking you to the doctor." I felt ashamed and thought, "Is God unable to get me through this? I trust Him, don't I?" I got up, showered, brushed my teeth, had something to eat and felt better.

The next day I went job hunting, but there were none to be had, so I decided to go back to school. I responded to an advertisement from British Columbia to study long distance to become a counsellor. That whetted my appetite to know more about relationships between people.

When that course finished, I signed up for the social service worker program in Toronto. I became hooked on helping people to manage their lives more efficiently through counselling.

Another five years went by before I went back to see my parents again. Mom had even more difficulty recognizing me, and for the first time Dad mentioned the possibility of Alzheimer's. Somehow, this visit actually ended up even worse than the previous one. Dad wanted me to see his side of the story, and I wanted him to see mine. I was demoralized. All my studies in counselling and how to communicate had done nothing to improve the relationship between my parents and me. What was I doing wrong? I wondered why I was even there and whether I had really forgiven them. Where was God in all of this?

I signed up with Tyndale University College and Seminary for the master of divinity degree, majoring in counselling. My professor was Brian Cunnington. His nonjudgmental understanding of human depravity and deep compassion for suffering people was pivotal in my understanding of forgiveness.

At the beginning of our third year, we needed to choose a subject to research and develop into a workshop presentation. Professor Cunnington gave us what seemed like an endless list of various topics, covering as many issues as could possibly come up in counselling. He added that if we wanted to research a topic not on the list, we had to discuss it with him so he could determine its suitability.

While my classmates were deciding between topics such as anger, divorce, crisis intervention, sexuality and anxiety, I was the only one out of roughly thirty students who wanted to research the subject of forgiveness. I introduced the idea to the professor, expecting him to refuse me.

"You want to write about forgiveness in a theological seminary?" he inquired. "Don't you know that people here already know everything there is to know about forgiveness?"

"I did wonder about that. I will pick one of the suggested topics from your list instead," I began, but he interrupted me.

"I'm being sarcastic," he said gently. "I *want* you to research and write on forgiveness."

"How many people before me have researched forgiveness?" I asked, trying to figure out how serious he was.

"Actually," he continued, "nobody here has researched forgiveness, because everyone thinks they know all there is to know about it. You are my first student to think differently."

It doesn't surprise me any more that many people think they know everything there is to know about forgiveness. Until my failed attempts at forgiving my parents, I too was convinced that I understood forgiveness clearly and fully. When pastors and other Christians assured me that I had forgiven my parents to the best of my ability, it didn't occur to me that there might be more to forgiveness than some churches frequently teach.

Forgiveness is not only a one-time decision or one single act, but also a process of many steps and many decisions. Not surprisingly, it may take years before it is finished. In one sense, forgiveness is an ongoing business, just like the brushing of teeth after each meal if you want to prevent cavities. Since emotions call the shots in how we interpret life situations and relationships, we need to explore their impact on us. We need to understand why they activate our responding behaviours the way they do. Forgiveness makes the work easier.

Section C
Constructing

Sin is not hurtful because it is forbidden. It is forbidden because it is hurtful.

Benjamin Franklin

A man who refuses to admit his mistakes can never be successful. But if he confesses and forsakes them, he gets another chance. (Proverbs 28:13, TLB)

Chapter 10

Forgetting What's Behind, Reaching for What's Ahead

It's said that to get something you've never had, you have to do something you've never done. I wanted to be reconciled with my parents, but up to now my efforts had fallen short of the mark. For much of my life I had avoided unpleasantness with them by distancing myself, emotionally as well as physically. In order to be reconciled, I would have to do something different.

I know that introspection gets a bad rap in some circles. And it's true that there is a danger that it will become self-indulgent, self-centred and self-absorbed. However, Lamentations 3:40 clearly advises, "*Let us examine our ways and test them, and let us return to the LORD.*" The key is to always return to the Lord—this will keep our self-analysis honest and our self-awareness God-centred. Living with bitterness, resentment and voices from the past, blaming others, and always excusing and defending our "self" is neither living God's way nor good for us. God wants us to be free from anything and everything that hinders us from knowing Him and living fully. In order to experience His freedom, we need to know and understand what those hindrances are, so we can sincerely and mindfully offer the whole of them up to God for removal.

***

Personally, as I worked through introspection and processed my strong emotions, I found strength and encouragement from Proverbs 28:13, "*He who conceals sins does not prosper, but whoever confesses and renounces them finds mercy,*" and James 4:10, "*Humble yourselves before the Lord, and he will lift you up.*" Fervently and sincerely, I started to pray Psalm 51 and Psalm 139:23–24, "*Search me, O God, and know my heart; test me and know my anxious thoughts. See if there is any offensive way in me, and lead me in the way everlasting.*"

I did a lot of journaling. As a result I wrote Mom a letter that I didn't send or ever intend to send.

Dear Mom,

You called me selfish and stubborn and hardhearted. I had to be all these things to survive and listen to the stuff children shouldn't hear. I wasn't your therapist or your friend; I was your daughter. I tried my best to be obedient and helpful to you. When you criticized me that I wasn't there enough for you, that I didn't understand you, that I was selfish and shouldn't have been born, it made me feel very bad about me, low and worthless and deserving of nothing good. When you blamed me for the things I didn't even do, I felt like there was no thread of good in me. It also made me so angry that I mouthed bad words behind your back. Today I know that you gave me of whatever was available to you.

I love you, Mom. I have always loved you...

The unsent letter helped me to speak out what was poisoning me inside and put closure on what happened between us. I asked God to forgive me and to forgive Mom also. Over time, my feelings of self-righteousness and entitlement to being treated "right" eroded. There came a day when I knew I had finally forgiven both of my parents and hoped to be reconciled with them again. I wrote them a letter different from all the previous ones and sent it immediately.

> *Hi, Dad and Mom,*
>
> *I am writing to you with a heavy heart. God has convicted me that I did not respect you the way I should have. He convicted me of bitterness and stubbornness. Even though a lot of water has passed under the bridge, I come to you with a broken heart, asking you to forgive me. Please forgive me for the things I did and of which I am ashamed today. Please forgive me for the things I said that were not spoken in love or with love. When I was young, I would have never imagined that I would cause such a terrible break between us and deprive myself of a relationship with people who mean so much to me. What can I do to reverse it?*
>
> *I love you both.*

For several months, there was no response from my parents. Christmas came and went with no acknowledgment of my letter or communication of any sort from my parents. Then, early in the spring, Dad called me. "I got your letter. That is all I want to say. I got your letter." He repeated that, perhaps out of fear of being misunderstood, or perhaps because he didn't know what else to say.

I asked him how he was, and how Mom was, and what was going on in their lives. The mood was strained and the conversation short. I asked if I could call again. "If you want to," he replied. I thanked him, and we said goodbye.

I called every week after that. We always spoke for only a couple of minutes, but slowly the ice started to melt.

That summer I was going to see my cousin, and I asked Dad and Mom if I could come and visit them as well. They both said yes. I resolved to go back for my third visit. I had been in regular phone contact with Dad for the previous few months, and I felt stronger in my faith and confident of a positive, albeit difficult, visit.

My sister, now remarried, picked me up at my cousin's, and we drove to the town where I had been born and where she and my parents currently lived. When we came to the house, only the dog came down to welcome us. Dad was waiting for us upstairs, since he now required a cane and was unable to walk as freely as he once did. Mom was asleep in her room. Besides eating, sleeping was all she did. Diagnosed with Alzheimer's disease, she no longer recognized me. She no longer spoke except to answer a direct and simple question, and she observed me as if I was a stranger. It hurt to see her like that.

I came prepared expecting the meeting to be tough. I wasn't prepared for just how tough. Dad blamed me for the twenty-plus years of lost time between us and for robbing him of the enjoyment of his grandchildren and great-grandchildren. In this he was right. I was careful not to discuss his contribution to it but took full responsibility for whatever part I had played in the situation. He was bitter about life so quickly coming to an end. It was heart-wrenching to see him, once so strong and athletic, now out of shape with a huge belly, chain smoking and drinking day in, day out. He was unrelenting in his blame towards me. Three or four times I said, "I know, I am sorry, please forgive me. You are right in what you say. I am sorry. Please forgive me." It seemed he couldn't get enough of hearing me say those words. As if he was questioning whether I really meant it.

Had God not been maturing me and growing my faith in Him in the safety of trusting and loving relationships with my husband and other people of faith, I might have reversed to the broken girl of my childhood, a shell drained of life from all that blame and accusations. But throughout the years God had taught me much about life from His perspective and about His love for all people, including my parents and me. I now saw Dad as a sinner not to be condemned but to be loved and forgiven. I wondered if the road to humility doesn't sometimes lead us through the jungle of humiliation. But God had better things in mind.

***

I went back to visit my parents a few more times, and we had some good times and some bad. Whenever we discussed neutral topics, the conversation went well. When my sister and I recalled the pleasant memories we had of growing up, it always made Dad feel merry and young.

The difficult times came with him questioning my Christian faith. I tried to be careful about what I said because by then I realized that I hadn't been as great an example as I had once perceived myself to be. However, my love for Jesus, and just the mention of His name, always upset Dad to no end. I could never get through the stubbornness of Dad, which Mom used to say I had inherited. We were so very much alike that we often clashed. He stood his ground, and I stood mine. It was during those days that I gained a new respect and understanding for Norman Cousins' words "Life is an adventure in forgiveness."

Because I couldn't deny Christ, Dad became very lukewarm towards me on what I thought was my last visit there. I resolved not to go back anymore, because the pain of disagreeing with Dad and seeing Mom changing into somebody I did not recognize hurt so very much. But the Lord had different plan.

***

In the spring of 2006, my sister phoned to let me know that she was taking Dad to the hospital. This was not entirely unexpected for someone his age who couldn't do without alcohol and cigarettes. I sensed I should go and see him, but I weighed my personal comfort against all such going entailed. I found excuses not to go: a) waste of time, and b) waste of money. What else could I expect but more of the same treatment and hollow arguments in the environment of chain smoking and drinking? I felt sick just thinking about it. Why should I continue to expose myself to it? The emotions from my childhood were reappearing again.

After Dad came back from the hospital he was in good spirits, and my sister commented that he would be around to torture her for at least another two years. I was glad to hear he was doing fine, and I kept in touch with him and my sister at least twice a week by phone, but at the same time I had this gnawing unsettledness that wouldn't go away. What if Dad died? Was he ready to meet his Maker and Judge? The thought would not leave me.

My desire to see Dad one more time and hold his hand intensified. One day my husband asked me directly, "Don't you want to go and see your dad? It's all right, you know, financially. Go if you want to; we will manage."

Though I was very tempted, I feared, among other things, being drawn into the same old conversations about how the Bible is full of lies and Jesus Christ was only a teacher and maybe a healer but not the Messiah, and definitely not the Son of God.

I remembered some of the things Dad told me about his childhood. His early memories as an altar boy were not encouraging. He spoke about being so poor that he had no shoes for the summer, only for the winter. The first summer Sunday he showed up without shoes to serve at the altar, the priest gave him a dressing down, and Dad ran away and never went back.

I myself had contributed to his attitude when I was about fifteen years old. I had picked up his mom's, my grandmother's, Bible and reading from the beginning "God created…" I started to call the Bible the most stupid book I had ever read, written by simple-minded people who didn't understand Darwin's theory of evolution.

"Do you really think that what is written in that book is a lie? My mother believed it." Dad was genuinely surprised and a little taken aback.

Because I loved my grandmother, I slowed down my spewing and pointed out that she hadn't gone to school and could barely read. Dad himself had never finished grade 7, but since I had made it to high school, he respected my opinion. My pronouncement against the Bible really influenced him.

How I am ashamed of those words now. I didn't know that the words we speak have the power of life and death. I spoke death to my dad, and I didn't even know it. What I would have done to take those words back. But the past cannot be changed, only the present, and only in changing the present can we hope to improve the future. I felt the walls of resentment starting to collapse. I chose to believe that God's love is powerful enough to overcome any adversity and to heal all hurts.

Chapter 11

Packing My Suitcase Again

In time Dad became more and more demanding of my sister's time, hardly willing to let her go out of his sight. I started to research airfares. It was peak season, and I felt that the ticket cost way too much. As I was contemplating the price, a question popped into my mind: "Do you love me more than money? Whom will you obey, the call of money or me?" Was this the Lord speaking, or was it my imagination?

Puzzled, I decided to call my sister, figuring that if there was any reluctance to my visit from her or Dad I wouldn't go. Secretly I hoped that neither of them would show interest in my coming.

Imagine my astonishment when Dad answered the phone. This was unusual. Ever since he had come back from the hospital in April, my sister had been the one to pick up the phone.

"Dad, do you want me to come and visit you?"

His answer surprised me. "Of course I want you to come. When will you be here?"

After that I spoke with my sister. "How do you think I can help you if I come? Personally I don't think I can be of any use."

Again I was trying hard to have her agree with me so that I could convince myself of the uselessness of my trip.

Her answer amazed me as well. "You are right, you cannot help me, but at least you will be here with me."

Taken aback, and without further excuse, I called the ticket agent and booked the flight in two weeks' time. Within half an hour the same agent called me back with a fare five hundred dollars cheaper if I left earlier and came back later. So here was the deal: I could get a better price, but I had to stay longer! I worried how I would last. I chose to trust that God knew best the reason for my earlier departure and longer stay.

***

In the days that followed I questioned whether I was like an abused woman needing to go back for more hurt in order to feel good. But really, that was not the case. I had worked through many of my issues, drawn sensible boundaries and was coming back altogether a different person. I felt powerless no more. I thought about what Jesus had done: He had come knowing He would be rejected and tortured by those He had come to love. He did it in order to give us that which we did not have and which, without Him, we couldn't even conceive of ever having—forgiveness and love. Jesus suffered the most abominable, vicious and wicked abuse of all because evil is powerful and can only be overcome by forgiveness and love. These two values, foreign to the world, could only be offered from the hand of God.

I decided to go back because God is love, and it was His love I wanted to share. I wasn't going there to judge, or preach or to justify myself. The motive was right. When I announced my decision to my daughter and a few faithful friends, they each affirmed me, saying, "God will bless your obedience." I wasn't sure how He would bless me, but I secretly hoped for a good job offer upon my return. In my eyes, that would be a nice payback for my obedience. What an earthling I am!

I sensed this was my dad's last summer. I wanted to hold his hand and tell him I loved him one more time before he died. For some reason, thinking about this stirs up a memory of my dad telling Anna and me about his dad—how he drank and was abusive to our grandmother, and how she had to work very hard all her life because her husband drank away the wages. Dad's parents were older when he was born; Grandma was forty and Grandpa was older.

Dad also told me about a woman he was in love with when he was only eighteen and who had his first child, a girl. Dad wasn't allowed to marry the child's mother or to keep the baby. His firstborn daughter was only a few years older than me. We met when I was seventeen. One day she knocked on our door, and when I opened it I was shocked to find a young woman who closely resembled my dad! She had been trying to find him and had finally tracked him down to our home, but he wasn't living with us any longer. I felt sorry for her and gave her some of my savings, but I wasn't able to help her beyond that. I was starting to understand why Dad felt cheated by life and probably by God, too.

My love for my dad was overshadowed by my fear of his dreadful temper. That, and memories of past visits, made it difficult for me to look forward to this trip. Whatever the outcome, however, I wanted to be obedient to what I sensed was God's invitation. I prayed that He would bless me with wisdom, compassion and love and help me to always be mindful of Him, my Saviour and my God.

A few days before I was due to leave, Peter got an emergency call from his boss. He was to fly out to California immediately on an assignment, even though he had just returned from there a few short days before. This added considerable stress to my final preparations, but I didn't have any control over it.

The day after my husband left for California, it was my turn to get on a plane. The evening before I was to leave, I logged on to the computer one last time and saw an email from my friend Ruth. It consisted of brief messages for each day that I would be gone—short writings in the form of meditations, excerpts from books and her personal prayers for me. We had prayed much for my parents, and she knew my heart was heavy. The email was her labour of love, a way of letting me know she would be thinking of me. I cried as I printed it out. The pages were more precious to me than gold, and I felt incredibly blessed and strengthened to be taking them with me on my trip.

Dear Zdenka,

You are on my heart this evening. I hope that I can connect with you before your trip. I would like to write a brief message for each day of your visit, kind of a sharing in prayer without the phone line. How glad I am that our precious Father will be the thread that draws us together across the miles. My prayer is that the miracles that He has done these past few months in your life will be "the markers" to know that He will be faithful in this new adventure with Him. You are so dear to me.

Love, Ruth

It was past midnight when I finished rereading the beginning sentences of Ruth's email, prayed for Dad and Mom, and again committed the whole trip to God. "Lord, You don't wish for anyone to perish, but for all to come to repentance. Thank You for giving me another chance to be with my parents. Lord, prepare their hearts, their minds and their souls to receive Your salvation. Break down the strongholds of pride, and open their eyes to see beyond this world." At the last minute, I felt a prompting to print out the lyrics to that old hymn "Just As I Am" in Czech. The format of Ruth's email gave me the idea to keep a daily account of my visit in the form of a diary, and what follows are my entries, beginning the day I left for Pearson International Airport in Toronto.

Chapter 12

Departure

Today of all the days to sleep in! I couldn't believe it. I stretched in my warm and comfy bed one last time, then quickly showered, ate breakfast, locked up the house, and started the drive to my daughter's. As I neared Brampton, construction on the highway slowed me down, and I knew I would be later than I had planned. "Whatever will be, will be," I sang under my breath. I thought about my son, whom I had said goodbye to the day before. How I loved my children and my husband! Briefly I thought about my own childhood and how my family had never really lived together. Even before the divorce Dad hardly slept at home. I had grown up disillusioned with the whole prospect of marriage and cynical about love. I realized then that I had never forgiven my dad for it. "I forgive you, Dad. Forgive him, Lord," I prayed on the spot and in my spirit.

I finally arrived at Claudia's, and she drove me to the airport, with the grandkids singing loudly in the back seat. On the way I read the first entry from Ruth.

Friday, June 23. Father, make my faith in what Your Word has promised so clear that the Spirit may work within me. Lord, strengthen and sanctify my entire will for the work of effectual prayer. This trip I give to You. I am faithful to go as You call me. The results are in Your hands. Amen. The One who calls you is faithful, and He will do it.

At the airport my five-year-old granddaughter Claire pushed a little envelope into my hands. "Here, Babi, read this on the plane and when you feel sad." My little darling! I kissed everybody goodbye and disappeared behind the turnstile. I was on my own now, alone with the books I had brought for the journey.

The plane was scheduled to leave in two hours, so I settled myself down in a lounge chair to read. Instead, however, I found myself looking around me, feeling very content, fulfilled, and proud. Here, in an international airport of visitors from other countries, I was, and had been for years, a Canadian citizen. I felt privileged to call this vast and wonderful country of Canada my home. I praised God for bringing me here and for leading me back to my parents, and even for the seven-hour flight ahead of me! I prayed in my spirit, "Lord, You are my God, the God who forgives and restores, who speaks truth and guides us into the fullness of life. Thank You for bringing me to this place of peace."

I realized that I was actually looking forward to being with Dad, Mom and Anna. I thought about the control issues that had come up for me again and again during the planning of this trip. I thought about when I was small and had no say over what went on in our home, namely the abusive treatment of my mom. I had felt responsible for her unhappiness and for Dad's actions towards her. No wonder that for years afterward I had tried to control whatever I could in my own life. Habits take so long to change, especially ones learned at a very young age!

Later on, high above the Atlantic and well into the flight, little children grew tired and settled down to sleep, either in

Departure

the cots provided by the airline or in the arms of their parents. While most adults were watching in-flight movies or themselves catching up on sleep, my mind went back to my first overseas flight, from Europe to Canada, and all the dreams that I had brought with me. Being young, I had hoped to change the world by my writing. Later, when I worked in the hospital, my supervisor once asked me what it was like living in a Communist country. When I told her, she dismissed my answer. "You were only eighteen when you left. How can you remember anything?" Then, when the Berlin Wall came down in 1989 and news about life behind the Iron Curtain started to make its way into the daily papers, magazines and TV, she grudgingly acknowledged, "It looks like you were telling the truth."

Has Jesus not spoken about how hard it is for people to believe the truth? In one of His parables He said, "*They will not be convinced even if someone rises from the dead*" (Luke 16:31). Truth is always challenging. I have discovered that, for the most part, people really don't like to be challenged in their established thought patterns, mostly because they don't like change. They stick to what they know, even if it isn't working for them.

How easily my thoughts ran on as the plane carried me quietly through the night. I had always enjoyed this sensation of floating through the air. It gave me the sense of being totally in the hands of my Lord, where nothing could harm me—not the past, not the present, not the future. Feeling secure in the love of the One who died for me made me long to be with Him and to look forward to a future place without pain or fear.

I opened the little envelope from my granddaughter. It contained two pictures she had drawn for me. In one, a man and a woman smiled at each other, probably my husband and me. On the other, a cat and rabbit, something she wished to have. There were blue waves all around, probably the ocean I was flying over. My little sweetheart!

After supper I did some reading and later watched the end of a movie.

The cry of a child made me glanced at my watch. I decided to catch a few winks before we landed. With people sneezing around me and another child crying in the back of the plane, sleep wasn't very restful. Soon I heard the announcement over the system to prepare for landing in less than one hour. People were waking up, the washrooms smelled, and the lineups for them grew longer. We were served coffee and a bun, and before long, the plane started to circle above Prague.

Chapter 13

Tracking the Days

Saturday, June 24. Drs. Cloud and Townsend, "When God makes a way for you through your trials, it is an active, not passive, process. God is active on your behalf, even when you cannot see it. And he calls you to be active also. At times, this may seem like a paradox to you. *Am I doing it? Or is God doing it?* The answer to both questions is "yes." God will do what only He can do, and your job is to do what you can do."[1]
"Trust in the Lord with all your heart, And lean not on your own understanding; In all your ways acknowledge Him, And He shall direct your paths." (Proverbs 3:5-6.)

In the afternoon. My sister had sent her husband to come and pick me up at the airport. He complained that she was very busy, staying at our parents' house 24/7. He worried about her.

"I don't know how long she can take this. She sleeps there, cooks there, eats there—she is there all the time. She fell, and her ankle is all swollen, but she doesn't want to go to a doctor. And the dog bit Mom's hand; it looks bad," Desi recounted, trying to prepare me.

Indeed, both of those injuries looked serious, and I urged them to go to the emergency department. Mom was given an antibiotic and told to come back in two days. Anna was given some pain medication and a tensor to wear for ten days.

Dad seemed to enjoy seeing me, and we hugged and kissed frequently. I hugged and kissed Mom too, but she didn't recognize me. My sister had calculated that Mom was entering her seventh or eighth year of Alzheimer's.

In the evening I sat outside with my sister, catching up on one another's lives. The night, soaked with moisture, released heat like an open oven. The polluted air prevented flies and mosquitos from breeding. No grass, only cement all around us. On my left was a large cement step, and to my right were a few iron steps leading to a little shop.

Suddenly, without warning, I felt the chair under me give way, and I breathed a quick prayer. "God, protect me! Don't let me break anything or have a concussion." It is amazing how much can fly through your head in a split second! As if in slow motion, I felt myself falling and saw my sister reaching out to help me. She suddenly stopped midway and simply stared at me as I continued my trip down. A thought flashed through my head: *What's wrong with her? Why isn't she helping me?*

When I got up, my sister asked, "What happened? You weren't even rocking in that chair!" I looked at the place where my head had landed, right between the cement step and the iron steps. An inch to the left or an inch to the right and I would have cracked my skull open. Amazingly, my head hadn't touched the cement ground, and there wasn't even a scratch on my elbows.

I thanked God aloud, and turning to my sister I asked her, "Why didn't you help me?"

In an awed voice she said, "It was the strangest thing watching you go down—as if a pair of hands was laying you down ever so gently."

"That's how I felt! It was as if angels were holding me and gently lowering me to the cement floor. It *was* the strangest thing. This is God!" I announced confidently.

Rejoicing, I took it as a reminder from the Lord that I didn't have to fear, because He was with me through thick and thin. I needed the assurance. I felt an unusual surge of strength and calmness. Peace like a river flooded my soul. I sensed that I had embarked on an adventure tour with my Lord. I felt Him to be very near, assuring me of His presence and love.

***

I sleep in my parents' house, downstairs in the same room with my sister. It is so good to be with her. As the clock is sounding the midnight hour, I look at her snoring softly beside me. How peacefully she sleeps, and what a life she had had! She had married shortly after her nineteenth birthday to a controlling man who beat her if she didn't do exactly what he wanted. Ashamed, she had hid it from me and told only my parents. They, too, were ashamed and hurting with her and hadn't told me either. I am starting to understand her more than I ever did before. Before I fall asleep I will claim this whole house, the house of suffering and shame, as I call it, for God and ask Him to fill it with His love.

> **Sunday, June 25.** Andrew Murray wrote, "Have faith in God, the living God. Let faith focus on God more than on the things promised, because it is His love, His power, His living presence that will awaken and work the faith."[2]

The mornings begin early in this house. Dad is usually awake before seven o'clock and needs to be taken to the bathroom. Mom keeps on sleeping. I wonder how I will be able to journal here. I will try the mornings or when Dad naps and probably finish at night. I shall see how it goes. Stop—Dad is calling me.

In the afternoon. Today I sang psalms and songs in English and Czech. Dad asked me about them, and I told him. He didn't stop me. At night my brother-in-law joined my sister and me. He heard about my fall to the cement floor yesterday and getting up, literally without a scratch.

"You are a saint," he said.

"Far from it! But God is great!" I laughed. He still insisted that I was a saint.

"If I am one it is only because God is making me into one." I replied.

Today I realized I forgot to pay our property taxes. God is teaching me to let go of control and fear.

Monday, June 26.

> St. Patrick's Breastplate
> I gird myself today with the power of God:
> God's strength to comfort me,
> God's might to uphold me,
> God's wisdom to guide me,
> God's eye to look before me
> God's ear to hear me,
> God's Word to speak for me,
> God's hand to lead me,
> God's way to lie before me,
> God's shield to protect me...

In the afternoon. Mom's hand and Anna's leg are healing nicely. Last night Anna and I talked about forgiveness and how I had messed things up with our parents. I shared with her my love for Christ, and she listened. Even though it was quite late, she said she didn't want to sleep, because she felt relaxed and energized with me there. What a compliment! Thank You, God. The glory belongs to You. Before coming, I had asked the Lord what the most important thing He wanted me to do in this place was, and He brought 1 Corinthians 13:13 to my attention: "*And now these three remain: faith, hope and love. But the* *greatest of these is love.*" Somehow, this time around, loving and serving are happening naturally.

In the evening. I am so tired. All I want to do is sleep! One last prayer that Peter will be able to fly home on Friday to pay the property taxes and Visa bill. James 4:2–3 says, "*You do not have because you do not ask. You ask and do not receive, because you ask amiss, that you may spend it on your pleasures*" (NKJV). In other words, our motives are wrong. I want the motives to be right, Lord, so whatever You deem necessary in this case, may it be so. You are able. I trust You. I exercise my faith rather than fretting, which, for me, is remarkable and different.

Tuesday, June 27.

"I am the LORD, the God of all mankind. Is anything too hard for me?" (Jeremiah 32:27)

The LORD is my light and my salvation—whom shall I fear? The LORD is the stronghold of my life—of whom shall I be afraid? (Psalm 27:1)

"Though the mountains be shaken and the hills be removed, yet my unfailing love for you will not be shaken nor my covenant of peace be removed," says the LORD, who has compassion on you. (Isaiah 54:10)

In the evening. Anna took a day off to see how I would manage our parents on my own before she went away for the weekend. I must say, I did well. The day was almost done when I settled Dad in for the night and came downstairs for my spiritual refreshment of prayer and Bible reading. It's past midnight. It's evening in Canada. I miss my home and my family!

4 a.m. A loud thump woke me up. I ran upstairs to see what happened. Dad had fallen while trying to go to the toilet by himself. His legs refused to carry him. It was awful to see him like this, helpless, not wanting to wake me up and trying hard to do those things for himself that he was once able to do. Skinny, his hands and feet shaking, he was a wreck of his former self. I bent over and tried to lift him up by myself, but Dad had no strength to help me, and I wasn't strong enough to lift him up by myself. I covered him with a blanket and called my sister to come and help me. She arrived shortly; we lifted Dad up from the floor and into his bed. We told him that he shouldn't go to the bathroom by himself anymore but should call us for help. Staring straight ahead, he didn't respond.

It must be very disheartening and humiliating for him to lose his faculties one by one, especially when he had been used to playing soccer and loved walking and running. Aging is a serious business for which we are definitely unprepared. Did I just hear the birds chirping? Is it possible it's morning already?

> **Wednesday, June 28.** From Max Lucado's *Next Door Saviour:*
>
> "Do you understand what God has done? He has deposited a Christ seed in you. As it grows, you will change. It's not that sin has no more presence in your life, but rather that sin has no more power over your life. Temptation will pester you, but temptation will not master you. What hope this brings!"[3]
>
> Blessings on your day with Him!

In the afternoon. A cousin of mine, whom I had the privilege to introduce to the Lord four years prior, is coming on Sunday and staying for three days to assist me with my parents as needed. She had cared for them on occasion during the last couple of years. Good news and good weather. Fantastic!

In the evening. I felt like singing a lullaby to Dad, the one I had made up for our kids when they were small. Tone-deaf as I am, when I started singing, Dad gave me the most precious toothless grin I had ever seen on anyone. How beautiful people look when you love them! I bent over him, held his hand and gave him permission to relax.

"Dad, you don't have to fight anymore; you can relax. You don't have to be strong any longer, and you don't have to be angry anymore. Let go of the pain, let go of your past, relax, and stop being on guard. Be the little boy you never had a chance to be."

With his eyes closed, his mouth drawn in a toothless grin, he reminded me of a little boy, safe and carefree at last. In liberating him I was liberating myself. Soon he was sound asleep, and I went downstairs to speak with my Lord. As I reflected on the day, the door suddenly flew open, and my nephew, my sister's twenty-one-year-old son, walked in and started a conversation. He talked about himself and his parents and my parents, his grandparents. I told him how I wished I had kept in touch with them, how one can never turn back the time, and how much better it is to think things through before one acts.

4 a.m. Dad called me to close all the windows. He was very cold, even though it was hot outside and the air inside wasn't moving. I was tired and I wanted to sleep, but instead I asked, "What else can I do for you, Dad?" He waved his hand. "Nothing else." I feel a deep love for him.

> **Thursday, June 29.** *"Now to the King eternal, immortal, invisible, the only God, be honor and glory for ever and ever"* (1 Timothy 1:17). The whole purpose of coming before the King is to praise Him. This morning I am praising Father with you. Know that I am lifting you to the One who is outside time and knows exactly what you have need of...So, praise Him!

I do, I do praise Him, dear Ruth! Peter called me from Midland and said, "They told me there is nothing for me to do right now and if I want to go home for a few days, I can. So I am home now." God has answered my prayer. I thank Him from the bottom of my heart.

***

Frequently I sit at the edge of Dad's bed, and he always moves towards the wall to give me more room. I think he likes it when I sit beside him and caress his hands. They are now so small, so thin, so purple and so cold. The other day as I caressed them, he reached for my hand as if to kiss it. I took my hand away and kissed his. He got upset and insisted on kissing my hand. So we kissed each other's hands and then I kissed his eyes and nose and forehead and cheeks. His toothless smile lit up his face once again. Peace and holiness permeated the room. I felt the presence of my Lord, and I cried tears of thanksgiving for His great mercy to me. I am having a great time with my dad. The best I have ever had in my whole life! Once again I thank God for giving me this precious, precious opportunity.

---

[1] Dr. Cloud H., Dr. Townsend J. *God Will Make A Way,* pg. 12. Nashville, TN: Thomas Nelson, 2002.

[2] Murray, A. *With Christ in the School of Prayer,* pg. 92 Springdale, PA: Whitaker House, 1981.

[3] Lucado M. *Next Door Saviour,* pg. 69. Nashville, TN: W Publishing Group, 2003.

Chapter 14

Just As I Am

Friday, June 30. Shalom means much more than peace. It means wholeness, completeness, finished word, perfection, safety, or wellness. *"So Gideon built an altar to the LORD there and called it The LORD is Peace"* (Judges 6:24).

In the morning. Today is the end of the school year, and children bring home their report cards. A report card was a big event for me. I wonder what report card the Lord would give me today for the life I've lived so far. I am so glad His mercy is everlasting and Jesus is my mediator! With Mom and Anna at the doctor, I will be alone with Dad most of the day.

In the evening. This afternoon as I sat beside him, Dad said, "This is it."

"I know, Dad. Are you ready?" I asked.

His lips started to quiver. "No, I don't think so," he replied quietly.

"Do you want to be?"

"I think so," he said after a while.

"I will read you something." I ran downstairs to get the song "Just as I Am," the one I typed out in Czech the night before I left for my trip. Only God had known the need for it.

Just As I Am
By Charlotte Elliot, 1835

Just as I am, without one plea,
But that Thy blood was shed for me,
And that Thou bidst me come to Thee,
O Lamb of God, I come, I come!

Just as I am and waiting not
To rid my soul of one dark blot,
To Thee, whose blood can cleanse each spot,
O Lamb of God, I come, I come!

Just as I am, though tossed about
With many a conflict, many a doubt,
Fightings within, and fears without,
O Lamb of God, I come, I come!

Just as I am, Thou wilt receive,
Wilt welcome, pardon, cleanse, relieve;
Because Thy promise I believe,
O Lamb of God, I come, I come!

What an incredible song! The truth of human life and salvation is laid out flat before one's eyes. The words in the Czech language are even more powerful. Dad cried from the beginning to the end. I had never seen him like that. Was it the Spirit whispering in his ears?

Dad and I talked about death and about God's love for every person. This time he didn't argue and didn't put me down. When I prayed, he even said Amen! Was it possible that Dad had now become a believer? What a blessing to be with my parents again!

Saturday, July 1. Happy Canada Day, Zdenka! I know so very little of the culture of your homeland...only the little you have shared with me. Today I pray that God will give you the opportunity to share with your family about the homeland that Jesus is preparing for all those who believe in Him. Oh, how I pray that their eyes will be opened, dear friend.

"In my Father's house are many rooms; if it were not so, I would have told you. I am going there to prepare a place for you. And if I go and prepare a place for you, I will come back and take you to be with me that you also may be where I am." (John 14:2–3)

You were once where your family is. Nothing is impossible with God. I see you smile! Celebrate your eternal home.

In the morning. How I miss Canada! How I miss my home! How I miss my family and my friends. I do not belong here anymore. Canada is now my home! Not because I have a Canadian passport, not because my permanent address is there, but because that is where my heart is. I anxiously count the days until I can go back to where I now belong. It hurts to be away from Canada, from my husband and from our children. The only thing that makes my stay here more bearable is that I love being around my dad, seeing my mom and having time with my sister. There is tenderness between us that I cannot remember ever being there before.

This is my second Saturday in Ostrava. Dad is becoming colder and colder, even in this unrelenting heat. I am sitting beside him, now my permanent position. I caress his very thin arms, hold his hands in mine and try to warm them with my own heat, all the time wondering if he still agrees to what we prayed a couple of days ago. I need to find out.

"Dad, it may be over soon. Remember, God loves you very much."

"Hearing it makes me so happy," he replied.

In the afternoon. God is showing me that no condemnation or naming of people's sins but only love and love alone can transform people. Doesn't the Bible tell us that God is love? His salvation and even His justice come out of His love. Love is above the law, which itself was preceded by His love. How would we know not to do the things that rob us of abundant life if His love had not revealed it to us through the law He gave? And again, it is His love that helps us to fulfill the law through Christ. It is His love that helps us to forgive others. Although we obey God's command when we forgive others, the truth of it is that forgiveness benefits us in the first place.

With the day finished, I rest before the Lord. While I ponder His Word I sense tension in the air. A thought comes to my mind, that Satan doesn't want to let go of his victim easily and is intensifying the battle. Inhaling a strange uneasiness about the place, I make a decision to fast and pray against the spirits of fear and lies and against the darkness itself not wanting to let go of my dad. Periodically he sees snakes around his bed. As soon as I pray, he calms down, but he still will not turn off his night lamp. Jesus, what else is needed? What bondage is my dad under? What are the hindering powers?

***

Only in God we can stand upright and have no need to lie

Only in God we will find the power to forgive and love

Only in God there is hope for every tomorrow

Only in God is life stronger than death

And high up in the sky I see the rainbow smile

What a gorgeous day!

What peace is mine!

Chapter 15

Your Face I Seek

Sunday, July 2.

These two things cannot change: God cannot lie when he makes a promise, and he cannot lie when he makes an oath. These things encourage us who came to God for safety. They give us strength to hold on to the hope we have been given. We have this hope as an anchor for the soul, sure and strong. (Hebrews 6:18–19, NCV.)

In the morning. Indeed, Lord, only in You alone there is hope. Your forgiveness brought me healing and removed the acuteness of painful memories. How glad I am for Your grace and mercy. What a difference being in this house today as compared to ten years ago! This time my strategy is love. Forget speaking about salvation or coming to Christ; convincing is the Holy Spirit's department. I am called to love "*with actions and in truth*" (1 John 3:18) Things get done as God works in us and through us and we do our part.

My theology professor at Tyndale, Dr. Shepherd, used to say, "There is nothing God cannot do without us, but there is nothing He will do without us." Souls can be saved and the kingdom of God realized only through prayer and acts of love. Now why has it taken me twenty-plus years to figure this out? "Because of the hardness of your heart" comes the thought, and it is immediately followed by another, that the hardness that protected me as a child became harmful to me as an adult. Bracing myself against the pain limited my openness to viewing life on a larger scale.

***

Seemingly out of the blue, a thought presents itself about Dad's bondage to cursing, unbelief, money, anger and lust. I feel the storm around me brewing and picking up speed. What must be done, Lord? I bow my head in prayer. "Lord, I seek Your face. You are the Lord, and there is no other beside You. In Your hands there is power and might. You are the victor, and the victory is in You! I kneel before You and in desperation of my soul I call unto You, knowing that You are able to save to the uttermost! You are my all in all, my salvation, the tower of refuge and strength; to You I run, to You I call! According to Your will based on Your mercy and Your love, show Your mercy to my parents and forgive their sins. Forgive my dad his unbelief in Christ caused by my inadequate modeling of Him who died for us. And forgive all who also modeled Christ to him poorly and wrongly. Include my parents in Your salvation and save their souls. You are the Creator of us all; nothing is impossible for You. I believe in Your never-ending forgiveness, and I trust in Your long-suffering love. Be gracious to us sinners, and pour out Your mercy and love! Yours is the glory, and power and might, forever and ever."

I am in awe of the invisible guidance of the Holy Spirit supplying me with incredible peace and joy beyond anything I have ever experienced so far. God indeed speaks! Only I have not yet learned the art of how to listen and discern. But slowly I am learning. I do what I sense I should be doing as long as it is not harming anyone and gives me peace. Taking step one without being able to see step two or three leads me directly to steps two and three. It is a new process for me.

> **Monday, July 3.** Andrew Murray wrote, "Do not simply *try* to believe the truths or promises you read. Your faith may then be in your own power. Believe in the Holy Spirit, in His being in you, and in God's working in you through Him. Take the Word into your heart in the quiet faith that He will enable you to love it, yield to it, and keep it."*

At noon. Yes, Lord. Purify and sanctify my heart, and work through me according to Your will. My cousin arrived last night to be with me as my sister leaves for her well-deserved mini vacation. Dad wet the bed twice. He doesn't make it to the bathroom anymore, doesn't want to eat, except for a few spoonfuls of soup and a little bit of yogurt. He mainly drinks water and sleeps more and more.

In the evening. The day passed uneventfully. About eight o'clock in the evening Dad called me into his room. He pointed his finger at the invisible snakes he said surrounded him.

"There are no snakes, Dad," I said.

He ignored me and pointed to the invisible fire on the floor and asked me to dump water on it. I encouraged him to trust Jesus. He relaxed, and I went downstairs. Once downstairs, my cousin and I read and talked about the Bible. She made some notes. It is two o'clock in the morning when we call it a day.

> **Tuesday, July 4.** "*Give thanks to the LORD, for his love endures forever*" (2 Chronicles 20:21). I'm praying that this day our precious Lord will put a song in your heart. Smile!

At noon. God loves me! He will not forsake me! The realization of it is sweeter than honey. Praise His name! Wonderful is His work. What a pity my parents were not able or willing to draw from His love. It was as if the painful, ugly memories in my parents' minds covered over all the good things that had also taken place. (The same was happening to me before I learned how to forgive fully.) Mom, perhaps still perceiving women as a personal threat, continued to prefer men and to try to please them. Even now, she often forgets my sister's name and mine, but she remembers the names of my husband and my sister's second husband! Or is it that dreaded Alzheimer's? It is maddening and sad and at the same time difficult to understand.

> **Wednesday, July 5.** Psalm 130. It is a lament psalm. Lament is complaining with confidence that God knows how we feel. Do you remember me telling you of Julie singing a lament at camp? It impacted so many that night. I am praying with you!

In the morning. What an encouragement today's note is to me! The weather is warm through the day and cooler at night. Perfect weather! Only Dad complains of freezing one minute and sweating the next. He sleeps either totally uncovered or with two thick blankets and a feather-down comforter. The bed is wet again this morning. My cousin and I manage to wash him and change the bed. He is now drinking through a straw while lying down. With the muscles in his body refusing to co-operate more and more, he doesn't have the strength to sit up.

---

*Murray, A. *The Blessings of Obedience,* Pg. 43. Springdale, PA: Whitaker House, 1984.

Chapter 16

A Night to Remember

Thursday, July 6. In the margin of one of my Bibles are these words: "Praise does not change my circumstances but it radically alters my viewpoint." *"Praise the LORD. Praise the LORD, O my soul. I will praise the LORD all my life; I will sing praise to my God as long I live"* (Psalm 146:1–2).

If you have time, read the rest of it. What a wonderful song.

In the afternoon. We go to visit our other cousin, a son of Mom's late sister. He is glad to see us. He's had polio since the age of two and walks on crutches. As he grows older the steel plates in his knees have to be periodically replaced, and now he has difficulty walking even with crutches. It is heartbreaking to think that as soon as he had barely learned to walk the freedom of movement was taken away. How I would love for God to heal him! I have prayed for his healing, asked others to pray for him too, but healing has not come, only the slow deterioration of his muscles and bones.

All day Dad slept peacefully. It is now close to midnight. Dad is calling me!

2 a.m. I am back. I was half undressed and writing in my diary when I heard Dad frantically calling my middle name—"Nina, Nina!"—the dear nickname of my childhood. I quickly zipped up my jeans and ran upstairs, taking two steps at a time. Running up the stairs felt like going through something thick and dark. I prayed quietly but out loud. I declared to the invisible world of the spirits that they had no power over me, because I belong to Jesus.

When I rounded the corner, I saw Dad lying in bed and pointing with his left hand in front of himself.

"Get him out, get him out!" he screamed at the top of his lungs.

"There is no one here." I tried to calm him down, without any effect. He wasn't listening.

He continued to scream, frightened by something I did not see. "Fire! Fire! Put out the fire! Put out the fire! Get him out!"

Suddenly I had a vision of Dad descending into hell. I reached for his hand and, with an authority that I had never used with him before, said very loudly, "Dad, you are descending to hell, and I cannot help you. I cannot help you! Do you hear me? Nobody can help you, only Jesus. I love you, but I cannot help you. Only Jesus can help you out from where you are going. Do you believe He is the Son of God?"

I was desperate. Knowing how Dad had refused to acknowledge Jesus as the Son of God before, I knew that this was his battle—a battle that I could not fight for him. Nobody could. A fight in the heavenlies was going on for my dad's soul, and only he had the power to determine its outcome. The crux of the matter tonight was the Lordship of Jesus Christ.

"Dad, you may not have much time. Do you believe that Jesus Christ is the Son of God?" I was sobbing and shaking all over. I was losing my dad, and there was nothing I could do to help him. This was it.

Dad didn't answer, but he relaxed a little. I felt spent.

Caressing his hand I said softly, "Dad, there is a fight for your soul, and nobody can help you; only Jesus can. Do you understand me? Do you believe that Jesus is the Son of God?"

Unexpectedly, after a moment or two, Dad stretched out in bed, hands limp beside his body, and said these amazing words: "It is a known fact that Jesus is the Son of God."

Had I heard that right? I almost fell off the chair.

"Do you believe that He died for you?" I asked.

Again, Dad had to think this through, and finally he said, "Yes."

I know that he spoke these words as a confession of faith and that they included Christ's crucifixion and resurrection in them, because this had been the whole point of contention between us. Hallelujah! I wept tears of relief and praised God for His enormous grace and love and patience and wisdom that He had extended to my dad and to me. I sat beside Dad, basking in God's goodness and grace.

At half past midnight, I felt strangely alive and not tired at all. About quarter to one in the morning Dad asked for a piece of bread. I wondered if he was hallucinating. I couldn't ever remember him eating dry bread, and especially not these days, when he was toothless. As strange as his request sounded, I figured, *Why not?*

I went downstairs to the kitchen and took out the bread, and I brought it to Dad. Bending over him, I said, "Here is the bread you have asked for. Do you still want it?"

"Yes, give me this bread."

As soon as the words were out, it dawned on me that he hadn't said "bread" in the everyday sense of the word but in the language that he used only at special, sacred times.

I remembered Dad's special relationship with the bread. Whenever he was home, before he made the first cut into the loaf of bread, he made the sign of the cross over it. What was the connection here tonight?

I broke off a small piece of bread and gave it to him. He opened his mouth and took the bread, almost in a holy way. Suddenly, it hit me. He was partaking of the Lord's Supper! I broke off a second piece of bread.

"Dad, the night Jesus was betrayed He took the bread, and broke it and said, *'This is my body, which is for you; do this in remembrance of me'* [1 Corinthians 11:24]."

I gave him the second piece of bread, and he took it gently in his mouth as a sacrament. It was a holy moment.

I said to him, "Dad, if I had wine I would now give you the wine, but I have only bread, so I am going to give you another piece of bread, as if it were the wine. So imagine this piece of bread is the wine."

Giving Dad the third piece of bread, I recited, "When Jesus took the wine He said, 'This is the new covenant in My blood, which is poured out for you. Do this in memory of Me.'"

Again, Dad, toothless, opened his mouth and took the third piece of bread with a sacred expression. After swallowing it, he moved his hand, signaling "Enough." It dawned on me that as a Roman Catholic, Dad was not used to taking wine anyway. For him this had been the type of communion he was used to.

A thought formed in my mind: *When Dad took the three pieces of bread, it was as if he had confirmed, affirmed and reaffirmed that he was now the Lord's—one piece of bread for each person of the Trinity. Awesome!*

I lingered on, holding Dad's hand, soaking up the holiness of the moment and pondering the awesomeness of God, who had entrusted me with the honour and privilege of leading my dad to Jesus Christ and how He, long before this moment, had strengthened me for the warfare required on my dad's behalf. Amazing! He had known what would take place, and He had totally prepared me for it. Praise His name! What a privilege, what an honour, to be in the presence of the Lord.

Long past one o'clock Dad squeezed my hand and said, "You spoke little, but you gave me a lot. Go, get some rest now."

I kissed him; he kissed me back. He reached for my hand and kissed it. I caressed his face. Then I went downstairs, still in awe, wishing for the beauty of this moment to last forever.

Wonderfully exhausted, I pray to God to awaken me should Dad need me again.

Section D
Developing

More things are wrought by prayer than this world dreams of.

Tennyson

Now to him who is able to do immeasurably more than all we ask or imagine, according to his power that is at work within us. (Ephesians 3:20)

Chapter 17

Mission Accomplished

Friday, July 7. Andrew Murray, "Amid the painful consciousness of ignorance and unworthiness, in the struggle between believing and doubting, the heavenly art of effective prayer is learned."[1] Christ is able...Praying that our God will be your family's God!

At noon. Indeed—Christ is able. Hallelujah! Dad is still sleeping. My cousin arranged to go home that afternoon. In the morning, my sister's husband took me to Ostrava to shop for our grandchildren. Claire had asked for a blue purse and Lucas for a wallet. I asked the Lord to help me find both items fast. And He did. The very first store had a blue purse small enough for our five-year-old granddaughter, and Lucas's wallet was in the next store! I got everything within the first few minutes. My stay had come to an end. Mission accomplished.

I walked through the city I used to call my own so many, many years ago. How things had changed! Mom used to call me an insensitive, proud and hard-headed mule. Was it truly me, or was it only a protection against the environment I lived in? Since I had only books and myself to guide me as a child, I grew perfect in my own eyes. After all, I was the smart one, I had straight As, I was the one to take care of Mom when Dad wasn't home and concerned for her when he was home, I was the one she asked for advice, I was the one who mediated issues between them, and I tried to smooth things out. I made myself not to feel and not to cry and to persist like a mule to be the best I figured I should be. I had plenty of reasons to feel proud of my accomplishments and abilities. The pride only intensified when I came to Christ. I saw myself as—righteous. Somehow I lost sight of the fact that only God is righteous.

When I finally admitted to myself the anger and grief I felt at being abandoned by my parents, I became ready to face my motives for having stayed away from them all those years. The one motive that unsettled me the most and took me completely by surprise was the realization that I wanted to punish them; I wanted to pay them back! Recognizing and admitting that I had harboured revenge in my heart against my parents and that I wanted to hurt them like they had hurt me was the hardest part of the work of forgiveness for me. It helped to read Romans 12:19: "*Dear friends, never avenge yourselves. Leave that to God, for he has said that he will repay those who deserve it*" (TLB). Although I had once fervently believed that my parents deserved punishment, I was no longer in the same frame of mind.

I believe that in the economy of God, the separation and the hardening of my heart served as a cast for my broken soul until I was ready to admit my brokenness, pride and anger, accept responsibility for my part in the relationship, and trust God for the results. The guilt I felt all those years started to make sense. On some level, I had known my vengeful attitude towards my parents was wrong. Although it felt good on some level to lash out at them from my hurting soul, there was never any peace afterward, just guilt.

If it weren't for the broken relationship with my parents, I might have never found out how proud and controlling I was, and that would have damaged the relationships I have with my children and grandchildren today. But God is able to bring good out of bad if we are willing to trust and obey Him. I would have also lost this most precious time with my dad, had I not obeyed the Lord and finally trusted Him with my broken heart. He had brought so much good out of so much bad. Praise His name!

> **Saturday, July 8.** Hal Urban, "We have the capacity to rise above the negative circumstances because we have a free will, the freedom and power to choose. Human beings weren't designed to live by chance. We were designed to live by choice."[2] I see your heart in it. I celebrate that we are forever family.

Dad still gets angry at times. The old nature in him doesn't want to die. But now it is enough to ask him, "Who do you belong to, the devil or Christ?" and his behaviour changes immediately. The change of the inner man takes time, and at eighty years of age there simply isn't time for the things that there used to be plenty of time for when he was younger. How long has it taken me? Let me count the decades…

My dear Ruth, I do not deserve your words. If I am changing, it is because of Christ's love and the love of people like you, my husband, my son, Michelle and Grace. No matter what I do, no matter how I fail, I can do no wrong in your eyes. That alone makes me want to always do better. And where would I be without my beautiful daughter, Claudia! Iron sharpens iron! Her birth, her little bundle of human perfection, had me seriously considering God for the first time. I wanted to know Him so I could teach her about Him, never guessing that she would teach me.

***

At the moment of birth, the biggest moment of life
When a new being is birthed through the agony of pain
At such a moment my love, my only one
Stay with me, please
For I am scared and all alone in this big hospital bed
Do not leave my side
In the life of every woman there are regions never visited by a man
Such is the moment of birth
When woman by herself
And with her
God

***

Sunday, July 9. "*That is why, for Christ's sake, I delight in weaknesses...For when I am weak, then I am strong*" (2 Corinthians 12:10). Dr. Henry Cloud, "Grace and truth give us the ingredients to head in the right direction and to provide the fuel we need to keep on growing and changing."[3]

I enjoyed a good half hour of praising and worshipping the Lord before I went upstairs. Dad was sitting on the edge of the bed, and I said, "Today is Sunday, and you haven't been to church for many years. I would like to read to you from the Bible. Would you like that?"

Dad said, "Yes, I want that."

Behold, a new man! This was not my old Dad speaking. My old Dad couldn't stand the Bible or Christ! As I read the ancient words of love in 1 John, Dad listened appreciatively and said thank you, twice. How unusual, coming from him!

"Dad, do you remember the story you told us one Easter about the two criminals who were hung beside Jesus? One of them made fun of Jesus, but the other one said, "*'Jesus, remember me when you come into your kingdom.' Jesus answered him, 'I tell you the truth, today you will be with me in paradise'*"

[Luke 23:42–43]. Dad, if you were to die tonight, you too will be with Jesus in paradise."

Dad wiped the tears from his eyes and said, "I am so glad."

> **Monday, July 10.** You are coming (or are) home. Rest in the fact that you were faithful to the job He called you to. I look forward to sharing with you. We will share the God moments and celebrate victories. Love, Ruth

The flight is uneventful, praise the Lord! I spend much of it thinking about this most recent visit and how, when I started to fast and pray in my parents' home, I prayed with new and different words, admitting to and confessing my sins against my parents, the hardness of my heart, my stubbornness and my lack of love for them. When feeling sorrow for one's sins goes hand in hand with humility and a turning away from those sins, repentance is real. How was this repentance different from the previous ones? Had I not been sorry for what had happened between my parents and myself? Certainly I had, but my sorrow extended only to grief and pain at how my parents had treated *me*, rather than at how I had treated them.

I considered what little I knew about my parents' childhood. Dad was hungry most of the time and had no toys to play with. My grandmother could spare him little time, because she had to work very hard to offset her husband's drinking. Once a year, she went to town to sell the baby goat and would come back with a gift for him—a crescent-shaped roll. Dad was hungry not only for food but for love as well, and he looked for it in all the wrong places.

Mom had grown up in only a marginally better family. Her dad worked night shifts in the coalmine and slept through the day. My grandmother gave preferential treatment to her much younger sister, and Mom was left to fend for herself. Neither of my parents had grown up in a nurturing family, and when they married they more or less continued the family culture. I had spent much of my life licking my wounds, and I had failed to see the wounds of my parents. T. Kempis said, "We carefully count others' offenses against us, but we rarely consider what others may suffer because of us."

Even though I had prayed for salvation for my parents and my sister, I never thought it would come to Dad. But God always hears us, and He answers in His time. If I had not connected with Ruth I would have stopped praying and hoping for good. It was she who kept plugging away at prayer after I had already given up.

She reminds me of a coach I had in grade school. As an eleven-year-old, I ran a 500-metre race with older girls. I was into athletics at the time and enjoyed it immensely. I remember starting strongly enough, but after 300 metres, which was the distance I was used to running up until then, I started to slow down and almost lost the main pack. Suddenly my coach came up beside me, talking to me, encouraging me and running with me. With his encouragement, my strength was renewed, I got my second breath, accelerated my speed and caught up with the lead group. I finished fifth among twelve- and thirteen-year-old girls and qualified for the next meet. Isn't that a description of God? He too comes alongside when we are tired and lifts us up, breathing His breath into us. With Him beside us we will always qualify for the next meet until we meet Him face to face. God doesn't want anyone to perish. His will is that all be saved. Don't give up on prayer and praying. God knows what He is doing. We only need to trust Him and keep on trusting, even if we cannot see the light at the end of the tunnel. Sir Winston Churchill said, "Never, never, never give up!" Most definitely, never give up on prayer! It's a stepping stone to freedom.

---

[1] Murray, A. *With Christ in the School of Prayer,* pg. 12. Springdale, PA: Whitaker House, 1981.

[2]Urban, H. *Life's Greatest Lessons,* pg. 36. New York, NY: Fireside Edition, 2003.

[3]Cloud, H. *Changes That Heal,* pg. 30. Grand Rapids, MI: Zondervan Publishing House, 1992.

Chapter 18

Love Overcomes

On July 13th I called my sister, after being home for couple of days, and she immediately commented on the changes in Dad's behaviour. She told me how he still got angry at times, but all she had to do was ask him who was winning, the evil angel or the good angel, and Dad would mellow right out. This was not the Dad we used to know! Anna told me she wanted what Dad had. I prayed with her. She asked me about the Bible and how to read it. (My trip was worth every penny!)

I kept in touch with her almost every day, sometimes twice a day. She said Dad was going downhill fast. He was often sleeping when I called. Sometimes I was able to tell him I loved him, and he said that he loved me too. I read to him from the Bible and sent him letters and tapes. My sister said that sometimes she heard Dad speak the name of Christ in prayer. She said that she read the Bible with her morning coffee. Sometimes we discussed her readings over the phone.

The power of God's Spirit is simply wonderful. What a privilege to work with Him in His vineyard! And the biggest wonder of all, the God of the universe wants to work with each one of us! It is for that purpose that He provides us with the much-needed skills by humbling us, not necessarily in a painless way but always in the way that is best for us.

On July 20th I read to Dad from Colossians 1:16–17: "*All things were created by him and for him. He is before all things, and in him all things hold together.*" The verses reverberated in me with a new potency. How mighty is our God! We can never comprehend Him. He is timeless, eternal. He reaches across the oceans, across the centuries, across the generations.

While I was in Czech I had found some loose pages from an old dream book and the following few words caught my attention. Translated they are as follows:

> Our spirit is the breath of the Holy Spirit of God for whom a thousand years is like a day and the past and the future is all in the present. The idea of everlasting does not describe time without an end, but rather describes existence for which there is no time. The most important things in life usually take less than a few seconds. So what is time when measured against eternity?

On August 4th I wrote a letter to my dad and sent it immediately.

Dear Dad,

I am thinking about you and I love you. Here is my prayer for you:

"*So do not fear, for I am with you; do not be dismayed, for I am your God. I will strengthen you and help you; I will uphold you with my righteous right hand.*" (Isaiah 41:10)

"*Fear not, for I have redeemed you; I have summoned you by name; you are mine. When you pass through the waters, I will be with you; and when you pass through the rivers, they will not sweep over you. When you walk through the fire, you will not be burned; the flames will not set you ablaze. For I am the LORD, your God.*" (Isaiah 43:1–3)

"*Before me no god was formed, nor will there be one after me.*" (Isaiah 43:10)

> *"Forget the former things; do not dwell on the past. See, I am doing a new thing!"* (Isaiah 43:18–19)
>
> *"Death has been swallowed up in victory. Where, O death, is your victory? Where, O death, is your sting?" The sting of death is sin, and the power of the sin is the law. But thanks be to God! He gives us the victory through our Lord Jesus Christ.* (1 Corinthians 15:54–57)
>
> I love you very much, Dad, and we are praying for you here.

On August 15th I called my sister to wish her a happy birthday. She said she read the letter to Dad twice the day before. "And a good thing, too, because today he isn't responding. He doesn't even know it is my birthday. I have mentioned it to him, but he doesn't react. His mouth is shut tight. It doesn't open anymore." She dissolved in tears.

We both sensed the end was near. Dad was on his way out.

***

The next day I went through childhood photographs as well as those from my last few visits to Czech. I was very weepy. I remembered Dad and the times we had spent together. This time I remembered only the good things. As I was doing dishes, I found myself whispering the words "God have mercy with his soul." It startled me, and I wondered if Dad had died. It was around 9 p.m. local time. It was about 3 a.m. at Dad's place. Although I wanted to call my sister, I did not want to wake her up. I decided simply to go to sleep, sensing more and more that Dad was no longer part of this life.

The ringing of the telephone woke me up about 1:00 a.m. Ontario time. My husband picked it up, but I was already wide awake and impatiently said, "Give her to me. The call is for me—it's my sister. Dad has died."

Peter, half asleep, handed me the phone, asking, "How do you know?"

Somehow I knew. Tearfully, my sister told me that Dad had died. She'd gone in to check on him at 7:00 a.m., and he hadn't responded. Then she saw he wasn't breathing anymore. The doctor confirmed that death had come early in the morning. My Dad indeed died on the brink of a new day—August 17, 2006.

That afternoon, as I was sorting through books in our basement, deciding which ones to get rid of, I discovered a red journal that I had kept for years. Out of curiosity, I opened it to August 17, and the entry took my breath away: "Dad called and woke me up around 6 a.m. to tell me that if I thought he was no good, then this would be the last time we talked. I said that we all have the freedom to do whatever we want. He hung up on me."

How amazing that years earlier, on the very same date my dad died, he had made a phone call that began what could have been the end of everything for our family. I had removed this specific phone call totally from my memory. Perhaps Dad tried to reconnect with me the only way he knew how, by starting a quarrel. Perhaps he was drunk that day. The idea had not occurred to me before. Only now did I remember that when I went back in 2004, Dad told me again and again that he had called me, and I kept saying that he didn't. How incredible, and what a strange coincidence, to discover this entry today, after all those years when I was so positive Dad never again tried to connect with me after that initial break-up call. Really, we only see what we want to see, hear what we want to hear and remember what we want to remember. God have mercy on us! Someone wrote, "Much of our pain is self-inflicted."

August 24, 2006. "Dad is being buried today," was my first thought as I awakened from my dream. And what an unusual dream I had had! I had seen my dad in a knee-length white robe, sitting on the bank of a gently running brook, looking intently into the water, deep in thought. I saw him in profile, and he looked very handsome and young and altogether in great shape.

Later, as I started the car to go to Barrie, I breathed in the beautiful summer morning and exclaimed, "I hope my dad is with You, Lord." Immediately, I heard in my spirit the exuberant words "I am, I am!" spoken in Czech. Instantly, and without a shadow of doubt, I knew that Dad had made it over safely, to be with the One who had given him life, not once, but twice. Praise be to our mighty God!

Chapter 19

Forgiveness for Me

It was springtime again. Only half a year had passed since my dad's death. Shortly before Christmas I had broken my right wrist roller-skating, and then towards the end of February I slipped on our icy driveway and hyperextended my knee ligament. It wasn't too serious, but it was very swollen, and I could not walk on it, so that is how my husband came to be whirling me around the grocery store in a wheelchair. I could barely read the labels on the shelves as he sped through the aisles, piling groceries into the basket on my lap. Pretty soon I saw nothing at all. And he didn't slow down! What's more, he had the gumption to tell me that I shouldn't be so uptight but just relax and enjoy the ride!

"Why are you so angry? It's just grocery shopping—and you don't even have to do any walking!" he said.

I was irritated and ignored him when he asked me what else we needed to get, deciding to give him the silent treatment. On the way home he told me that I was angry just like my dad when I did not get my way. That hurt.

When we got home I decided to make cream of wheat with blueberries for supper. As I cooked it, I remembered one very cold night, either in the spring or fall, when my mom, Anna and I were coming home from my mom's parents. They had wanted us to stay and spend the night there, but Mom was afraid of what would happen if Dad came home and didn't find us there. So we went home on the late bus, and my sister fell asleep. Mom carried her because she was two years younger than me, and I had to walk. I remember wanting to be carried too, but Mom explained that she only had two hands. To give me the initiative to walk that long trek from the bus station to our apartment, she promised to make cream of wheat for me when we got home. I loved cream of wheat.

After we got home and Mom put Anna to bed, she started to cook supper. I was tired and not really hungry anymore. When the cream of wheat was finished cooking and Mom put it in front of me, I started to criticize her for the lumps she hadn't stirred properly, all the while thinking that I sounded just like my dad and how awful it was. Yet I couldn't stop myself. The more Mom tried to calm me down, the angrier I grew and the more I criticized her. Through tears she told me I was just like Dad, torturing her in his place. I felt horrified seeing Mom unravel like this, but I had no words with which to express my sadness or my regret at how deeply I had wounded her.

***

As I cooked the cream of wheat and thought about what has transpired at the grocery store, I started to weep. For the first time in my life I connected the frustration and anger I had as a child to missing my dad, who was so seldom with us. The anger I dished out at Mom that night had really been anger at Dad because I missed him so very much.

When I shared this with my husband he was quiet for a few minutes and then said, "Remember how I asked you why you were so angry? I couldn't understand why you've been acting like your dad lately. Now I do. You're still missing him."

My husband's insightfulness helped me to identify yet another root of my anger. At the same time, however, remembering that evening with my mom brought back feelings of deep shame at the hurt I had caused her, and I thought about how she and I never seemed to be able to connect or talk things through.

When I first came to know Jesus Christ, I shared my faith with both of my parents, but I never knew if my witness had any effect or influence on Mom. I never asked her if she was able to find encouragement in God. Throughout her life she always said that every road leads to God, but the experiences with my dad confirmed what Scripture says, that although perhaps many roads lead to Jesus Christ, only one leads to God—and that road is Jesus Christ, His Son. Unfortunately, I never had the opportunity to discuss it with her. Soon after Dad's death Mom's mind went into a steep decline. She was unable to even feed herself, barely managing to swallow when spoon-fed.

Although I never had the opportunity to witness to my mom in those final years of her life, I was deeply moved and comforted by a disk of video clips that Anna had recorded just before Mom went into a nursing home.

One of those clips showed Mom with her head bent, hands together and fingers intertwined. My sister asks her, "What are you doing, Mom? Are you praying?"

"Yes, I am," says Mom.

"Can you pray aloud?" my sister invites her, and Mom prays the entire Lord's prayer.

After she finishes, my sister says, "I'm going to send this to Zdenka, your firstborn daughter. Is there anything you want to say to her?"

Mom is quiet, looking like she has withdrawn into her own little world. Then slowly she says these incredible words: "Tell her I love her."

"You tell her that," insists my sister. "Just say it."

And so Mom says, "I love you, Zdenicka."

She remembered my name! She said the words I had longed to hear from her all of my life. For one brief moment she remembered that she had a daughter named after her. With that simple expression of love, all pain was forgotten in an instant. Love alone remained. I love you too, Mom. I have always loved you.

***

On October 9th my friend Michelle came for a visit, and the next day we both went to see Grace. Around noontime we started to pray. I prayed that God would accept my mom into His kingdom.

In the evening, as Michelle and I drove to Barrie, where I was facilitating the 12 Step Spiritual Journey group, right there on the highway I started to cry as my thoughts drifted to Mom. And once again I said those words: "Lord, have mercy with her soul." This caught me off guard, and I wondered aloud if Mom had died. Michelle was puzzled and tried to assure me that it was only because we had been thinking about and praying for Mom throughout the day.

The next day my sister called me at 8:00 a.m. to tell me that Mom has indeed died during the night. Mom died on October 11, 2007.

***

For the longest time I regretted not obeying God's first prompting, years earlier. The guilt and shame about what I failed to do was twisting my view of God and who I was in Christ. During the peak of my struggle with this guilt before

God, He reminded me of Matthew 21:28–31, where a father asked his two sons to go to work in the field. The older one said no, and the younger one said yes. But at the end of the day the younger one didn't go and the older one changed his mind and went. Which of the two was obedient? In God's kingdom even late obedience is still obedience. What stopped me dead in my "guilt-track" was 1 Corinthians 13:5: Love "*keeps no record of wrongs.*" When God, who is love, keeps no record of wrongs, why should I? Focusing on guilt leaves me no energy to focus on God's grace. Being consumed by what I didn't do takes time away from praising God for what He enabled me to do. Finally I realized that just as I cannot blame a cat for being a cat and doing what cats do, in the same way I am a sinner who sins, and only with God's help it will happen less often. God understands that life is difficult and painful. He loves us, and He forgives us each and every time we come to Him in faith and sincere repentance.

Not everybody in our lives will extend forgiveness to us when we ask for it, but God forgives all who sincerely desire to be forgiven. God holds no grudges. God does not exclude anyone. Even if your sin seems too big to you, remember, "His power to forgive is much bigger than your power to sin." God bless the heart of the one who said it. When we insist that our sin is too big for God to forgive, we make Him a liar and make ourselves more righteous than He is. How do you like that?

For some it's very difficult to appropriate God's love and forgiveness for themselves. It was for me. Yet the Bible says in Isaiah 43:25 that God blots out our transgressions for His own sake. For His own sake he cleanses us. He cleanses us so we can be in relationship with Him. Isn't He awesome? Let us trust Him! Let us receive His forgiveness. Let us receive His love. Let us do it with faith, for "*without faith it is impossible to please God*" (Hebrews 11:6).

The more truth we learn about our Saviour, the freer we become, and the freer we become, the more truth we learn about ourselves and others, and our faith grows exponentially.

***

Forgiveness is of the utmost importance in the life of a Christian and the number one emotional healing tool for all people, but some don't realize how much more there is to forgiveness beyond saying "I forgive." True forgiveness is very much like an antibiotic—the course of treatment must be completed and seen through to the end. Otherwise the cure is incomplete and leaves us vulnerable to further illness. An incomplete, half-baked forgiveness leaves us stuck in the past, rehashing old hurts, reopening painful wounds, and keeps us in a vicious cycle of self-destructive behaviours. If we try to bypass our emotions instead of acknowledging them and evaluating their validity, it will be like pulling out weeds by the stems and leaves but leaving the roots buried and alive. The roots will continue to reproduce and keep us imprisoned by our past.

It was only after I faced and admitted the bitterness and sorrow and anger in my own heart that I was able to bring them before God for forgiveness. Forgiveness can also be viewed as the pruning of the dead branches so new growth can appear, bearing good fruit in us like "*love, joy, peace, patience, kindness, goodness, faithfulness, gentleness and self-control*" (Galatians 5:22–23).

I can choose to hang on to my guilt and shame for the way I was with my parents and to spin in a cycle of pain and defeat. Alternately, I can choose to be released from guilt and shame by accepting the forgiveness God offers in Jesus Christ. My parents' choices kept them in a vicious cycle of abusive ways of relating and dragged Anna and me into that same cycle. Were it not for the power of the cross to interrupt that cycle and raise me up to a new way of living, I would have had no hope of escape. The same way that my parents' choices affected me, so my choices today affect my children, and my grandchildren. I am so thankful to God that it will be for good, and not evil. It is very freeing to know that God has forgiven me and that He loves me!

Reconciliation sometimes happens as a result of the forgiveness process, and it is always a two-way street, while forgiveness is not. We don't need the other party to forgive us in order for us to forgive them. It's wonderful when that happens, but we don't have any control over it. Not everybody will be as successful as I was. But the Bible is clear: "*If it is possible, as far as it depends on you, live at peace with everyone*" (Romans 12:18).

To be able to do that, we must first live peaceably with God and then with ourselves in our innermost being. First John 4:8 tells us that "*God is love.*" When God offers forgiveness, He offers of Himself. Forgiveness is love offered and acted out. When we accept His forgiveness, we drink of His love. When we don't accept His forgiveness, we reject His love and try to satisfy our thirst for it in unhelpful ways.

Forgiveness reveals God's love to us the best. It is also the best way to pass love—God's and ours—on to others. Look at forgiveness as a recycling depot. We bring in our character defects and our mistakes, and they get recycled into something valuable and beautiful, like tenderness, compassion, understanding, grace, mercy and love. I realize that everything I had wished had never happened has turned out for the best because of God's love and forgiveness. But I had to make the choice whether to live in the perpetual conflict of self-righteousness and bitterness or in the freedom of forgiveness and grace. You too have the same choice. Will you choose the freedom of forgiveness or the slavery of conflict? Your choice will direct your life. Choose carefully; your freedom and your health (physical, psychological and spiritual) depends on it.

Limping Through Forgiveness

Archbishop Desmond Tutu was awarded the Nobel Peace Prize in 1984, and in 1999 his book *No Future Without Forgiveness* was published in New York by Doubleday. His address to the new democratic South Africa, published by the University of Wisconsin Press in spring 1995, included this:

> Without forgiveness there is no future. Forgiveness is taking seriously the awfulness of what has happened when you are treated unfairly. Without forgiveness resentment builds up in us, a resentment which turns into hostility and anger. Forgiveness is not pretending that things are other than they are. Forgiveness is not cheap. It is facing the ghastliness of what has happened and giving the other person the opportunity of coming out of that ghastly situation. Forgiveness does not mean amnesia. Amnesia is a most dangerous thing. We must forgive, but not forget that there were atrocities, because if we do, we are then likely to repeat those atrocities. If we don't deal with our past adequately, it will return to haunt us.

We live in crazy times. Mental illness is on the rise, as are the rates for suicide, homicide, divorce, abuse, self-harm, use of drugs and a number of other concerns. I can't help wondering what the world would look like today if Christ hadn't come to teach us how to love. His ideas are as startling and revolutionary today as they were two thousand years ago. Jesus said that only the truth would set us free.

Here is the truth: only One was called the Son of God and the Son of Man. Only One was crucified, buried, and came back to life again. His body was never found, but many had seen Him alive and well. What do you make of that?

As for those who would believe that we live in a world of illusions only and that nothing we see or experience is real, I can only say that I will never forget the fear Dad had that night he saw fire on the floor and a stranger in his bedroom. Although I saw nothing, he was convinced it was real. Was it a simple hallucination? I certainly wasn't able to talk him through it or reason him out of it. It was only when I brought Jesus into the situation that things changed.

The reality of the change that I saw in Dad when he confessed Christ as the Son of God was as incredible as it was undeniable. The transition from terror to complete peace was not an illusion. The fact that he stopped using his nightlight from then on was not an illusion either. To me this was a witness to the reality and power of Jesus Christ, who said, "*I am the way and the truth and the life. No one comes to the Father except through me*" (John 14:6).

The Bible must not be taken lightly. Its principles have stood the test of time. Even today's psychology, and all that is good in it, derives from it. The biblical principles will not be obliterated, but if we go against them we will obliterate ourselves. How do I know? I know it from my own personal experience and from the testimonies of countless others. As a counsellor, I come face to face with the pain and sadness of broken families every day. From their stories I know that human beings want to be happy. It's clear that the coping behaviours of sex, substance abuse, self-harm and others don't bring them the happiness they are looking for, only more turmoil and bigger problems.

In my own family of origin I suffered the devastation caused by some of those "self-managing behaviours." I came to Canada looking for freedom and realized that I carried it within me! It's the freedom of choice. Use it wisely. I did and chose Christ—the One from whom all freedom flows. He has proven Himself to be more than enough for every circumstance in my life.

How about you? How free are you? What might you be in bondage to? And what fears might be keeping you in that bondage? Think about it. "*There is no fear in love; but perfect love casts out fear, because fear involves torment*" (1 John 4:18, NKJV). How very true. I believe that fear and love are the two primary emotions. If there is one, there is no place for the other. Everything negative comes out of fear, and everything good and perfect comes out of love, because God is love, and He "*has not given us a spirit of fear, but of power and of love and of a sound mind*" (2 Timothy 1:7, NKJV).

Fear expands astronomically without Christ. Only love of God is strong enough to keep a check on it. Are you filled with His love? Do you have difficulty believing that God can love you? You are not alone. As I was praying about this book the other day, I asked the Lord why it is still so hard for me to believe that He loves me. A thought about my childhood came to my mind, and like a little pebble thrown in a quiet lake it slightly ruffled my memories. I said, in total awe and yielding to my Lord, "I love You, Jesus. I love You so very much!" And right away the words came to me: "Only because I loved you first." It was in that instant that I fully comprehended the power and the depth of His love. *We love Him because He first loved us* (1 John 4:19). It's that simple and yet so hard to understand and believe.

I pray that God will reveal His love to you in a special way. Thank you for investing your time in reading my story. I hope it has encouraged you in your own forgiveness journey. When you do it with God, it will come out right. Be blessed!

***

Forgiveness for Me

I was falling, falling, falling
When God put His mighty arm around me and
Caught me
I was hurting, broken and dirty
When He made Himself real to me
I knew then
His love can heal
He made me whole again and
Without a fanfare
I decided to trust Him
Like I have never trusted any friend
To trust
To live
Jesus my Lord
Jesus the mighty King

Appendix
Stages of Forgiveness

"In a time of universal deceit, telling the truth is a revolutionary act."

George Orwell

"Then you will know the truth, and the truth will set you free." (John 8:32)

Stage A

Admitting

This stage is about admitting and grieving what happened between you and the other person. It helps to keep a journal throughout this process. Begin by recording what happened, where it happened, when it happened, why you think it happened, how you felt about it and what went through your head. Include your feelings, thoughts, corresponding actions or reactions, and any unfulfilled longings or broken dreams you had or still have for the relationship. Allow yourself to remember other situations in your past that have affected you in a similar way. Journal your responses. Here are some questions to get you started:

Q: What's your story?

Q: How has it affected you?

Q: At which point in your story have you become stuck?

Q: How is it affecting you?

Q: Have you at any time responded in a way that is now disturbing you?

Q: Are you able to share this experience with another person?

Q: How do you feel about facing it *now*?

Q: How would you prefer things to be different?

Q: What would your life look like if things were different?

Q: How willing are you to start the forgiveness process?

Q: Is there anything you are afraid of admitting?

Stage B

Becoming

This stage is about becoming—you'll have to choose whether to become an overcomer or remain a victim. This will involve recognizing your contribution to the conflict and separating it from the other person. Here are some questions to help you in this stage:

Q: How do you think your life will be affected if you don't forgive?

Q: What might your life be like if you forgive?

Q: What would you rather be, a victim or an overcomer? (If still undecided, go back to stage A and continue processing your emotions. If you feel stuck, get some help from a professional.)

Q: How might your behaviour be different if the situation hadn't happened?

Q: How might your life be different if the situation hadn't happened?

Limping Through Forgiveness

Q: Are you open to the possibility that your current perception of the situation may be biased?

Q: Are you willing to reframe any misconceptions/any bias?

Q: What are you willing to reframe?

Q: How can you reframe it positively?

Q: How will the situation, relationship, or any problem look once reframed more positively?

Q: Are you noticing any changes in your feelings and thoughts about what happened?

Q: What are you slowly becoming aware of?

Stage C

Constructing

This third stage is about constructing a new understanding of forgiveness and tearing down old attitudes. Here are questions to help you along:

Q: What do you think and how do you feel about this stage?

Q: What is the motivating force behind those thoughts and emotions?

Q: Which one of your thoughts are in need of adjustment or a total reconstruction?

Q: What does the Scripture say about forgiveness and do you believe it? (If your answer is yes, please continue with the next stage. If undecided, please see a person of faith to help you wrestle through the issue.)

Q: What have you learned that helped you to understand your situation in a new way?

Q: How is it helping you with reconstructing of what was, but *now* doesn't have to be?

Q: In constructing a new concept of forgiveness—what must be left behind?

Q: On what principles are you *now* constructing your new understanding of forgiveness?

Stage D

Developing

Stage four is about developing new experiences and an improved understanding of people. It's about offering grace and extending forgiveness, not only to others but also to yourself. True, not everything is only our fault, but the minute we realize our contribution to the situation we must try to correct it from our end. Here are questions to help you along:

Q: How does it feel now to think in terms of forgiveness for others and yourself?

Q: What thoughts and feelings are coming up inside you?

Q: Is there still something preventing you from taking this step? (If it's anger or guilt, please reread chapter 19.)

Q: Who in your life stands in need of your forgiveness and God's grace and mercy?

Q: What will you do about it?

Q: When will you do it?

Q: What do you plan on doing to keep on developing this understanding of forgiveness?